CW00506242

Yours Truly,
J. C. F. Kyger.

ELOCUTION SIMPLIFIED

OR, HOW TO

READ AND SPEAK

CORRECTLY AND EFFECTIVELY.

CONSISTING OF A THOROUGH AND PRACTICAL TREATISE ON GESTURE, VOCAL
CULTURE, INTONATION AND CALISTHENICS.

PREPARED FOR

THE USE OF SCHOOLS,

AND

FOR PRIVATE INSTRUCTION.

BY

J. C. F. KYGER,

OF SAVOY LITERARY AND COMMERCIAL COLLEGE.

CLAREMONT, N. H.
CLAREMONT MANUFACTURING CO.
1884.

JUL 30 1904

160970

PN4111
.K9

Entered According to act of Congress, in the year 1883,

by J. C. F. KYGER,

in the office of the Librarian of Congress, at Washington.

DEDICATION,
By
The Author,
To
Those Who
Admire the Grand
and Divine Art of Elo-
cution; To All Who would Im-
prove the Commerce of the Soul; And
to All Who would Endeavor
to Give to Thought Its
Highest Mode of
Expression
This
Little Volume
Is
Sent Forth on Its Mission of Proposed Usefulness,

INTRODUCTION.

In the following pages, it is the aim of the author to bring before the mind, in the most simple and concise manner, the *much neglected Art of Elocution*.

The following are some of its special features.

1. The *definitions* are plain and short, yet conveying the true meaning.

2. The *divisions of the subjects* are arranged for blackboard exercises, as they are fixed more firmly on the mind, when brought before the eye.

3. Under each subject, *appropriate examples* are furnished, which impress more firmly the idea conveyed by the definition.

4. In the most difficult parts of Intonation, the *philosophy of voice* is given. Thus the student may, at once, see the manner of producing tone, and he is not left merely to wander in the realms of his own imagination.

5. A table of exercises in *Vocal Gymnastics* is given for the frequent practice of the student, as it is impossible to secure free use of the organs of speech, without good and easy respiration.

6. The subject of *Gesticulation* is mostly presented in diagram, which is the most effective way of expressing a thought. Thus, the vivid images of the subject are delineated to the student and they become, as it were, creatures of his own mind.

After extending his most grateful thanks to all who have aided him in any way, either in the arrangement or publication of this little book, the author will say that, if it shall add another trophy to the modern march of mind, or shall cause one holy aspiration of the *noble and divine science and art of Elocution* to flit across the mind of anyone who shall read these pages, he will feel himself many times repaid for his unceasing toil in its preparation.

J. C. F. KYGER.

Denison, Tex., April 1, 1884.

TABLE OF CONTENTS.

10 TABLE OF CONTENTS.

PAGE.

"Thoughts must breathe before words can burn."

"The heart must glow e'er the tongue can gild."

"There's a charm in delivery, a magical art,
That thrills, like a kiss, from the lip to the heart;
'Tis the glance,—the expression,—the well chosen word,—
By whose magic the depths of the spirit are stirred,—
The smile,—the mute gesture,—the soul stirring pause,—
The eye's sweet expression, that melts, while it awes,—
The lip's soft persuasion—its musical tone :
Oh! such were the charms of that eloquent one!"

ELOCUTION SIMPLIFIED.

Let it not be said that

ELOCUTION

Is only the tinsel of Eloquence. Demosthenes justly deemed a correct delivery the very acme of the art, and devoted to its acquirement years of toil and thousands of gold. Cicero applied himself to the cultivation of the vocal powers, under the most eminent instructors with unwearied assiduity. Chatham practiced before a mirror daily to the end of his life, to acquire a free, graceful, and energetic action. Brougham locked himself up for three weeks to the study of a single oration, and wrote his peroration fifteen times. Robert Hall, the prince of pulpit orators, was no less remarkable in his early life, for his laborious culture of Elocution, than for his profound philosophical investigations. Similar remarks might be made of Chrysostom, Massillon, Whitefield, and all who have distinguished themselves in the "*art divine.*" Would we realize their success, we must imitate their example. "He who enters the arena of eloquence without cultivating his elocution, has seized a sword for the contest, upon which he has put no edge."

ELOCUTION

Is the Science and Art of Expression.

ELOCUTION { VOICE.
{ GESTURE.

IMPORTANT DEFINITIONS.

The SOFT PALATE *is the partition between the nasal and vocal currents.*

The UVULA *is the pendant portion of the Soft Palate.*

The GLOTTIS *is the upper portion of the Windpipe.*

The PHARYNX *is the open cavity between the Glottis and Soft Palate.*

The LARYNX *is the Windpipe in the throat.*

VOICE

Is the principal material of which speech is made.

How Produced { By emitting breath from the Lungs over the
{ Vocal Membranes, or Vocal Cords.

BREATHING

Is inhaling and exhaling air.

BREATHING
1. DEEP.
2. ABDOMINAL.
3. COSTAL.
4. DORSAL.
5. WAIST.
6. EXPULSIVE.
7. ABRUPT.
8. EFFULSIVE.
9. PROLONGED.
10. UNEQUAL.

I. DEEP BREATHING.

Position.—Arms Akimbo.

First.   Inhale a deep breath slowly.
     Inhale through the nostrils.
     Avoid raising shoulders.

Second.   Give out breath through the nostrils.
     Hold chest expanded with easy firmness.

II. ABDOMINAL BREATHING.

Position.—Arms Akimbo.

First.   Inhale through the nostrils.
     Abdominal Walls thrown outward and convex.

Second.   Expel breath through nostrils.
     Abdominal Walls drawn in and flattened.

III. COSTAL BREATHING.

Position.—Palms of hands against lower ribs.

First.   Inhale through the nostrils.
     Expand the waist sidewise.

Second.   In expelling, contract waist sidewise.

IV. Dorsal Breathing.

Position.—Hands at waist, thumbs forward and fingers pressing against the small of the back each side of the spine.

First.   Throw out muscles, where fingers rest, while inhaling air.

Second.   To expel air, draw muscles inward.

V. Waist Breathing.

Position.—Hands at the waist, fingers thrown forward.

First.   In inhaling, expand the waist in all directions, as if bursting a belt.

Second.   Contract waist and expel breath.

VI. Expulsive Breathing.

First.   Inhale through the nostrils.

Second.   Expel through the mouth, as if whispering the syllable hoo! to a person at-a distance.   Give out breath in a firm full column.

VII. Abrupt Breathing.

First.   Catch breath quickly, through nostrils.

Second.   Emit air with sudden whisper—"hoo!"

VIII. Effusive Breathing.

First.   Inhale a full breath.

Second.   Expel through open mouth.
Prolong the sound of the letter "h".
Make a gentle breathing murmur.

IX. Prolonged Breathing.

First.   Draw in air easily, through contracted lips.

Second.   Breathe out the air, through nearly closed lips, slowly and gradually.

X. Unequal Breathing.

Position.—Place the palm of the left hand, against the side,
    close under the armpit.

Bend the right arm directly over head.
Practice deep breathing in this position.
Reverse this position of arm, and repeat.

NOTE. The foregoing exercises should be practiced often, as it is impossible to
secure ease and clearness of speech, without proper breathing.

ARTICULATION,

Good or bad, is the utterance of the Oral Elements.

ORAL ELEMENTS *are the sounds that form syllables.*

ORAL ELEMENTS ARE PRODUCED *by the voice and breath coming
    in contact with the Organs of Speech.*

THE PRINCIPAL ORGANS OF SPEECH *are the lips, teeth, tongue,
    and palate.*

ORAL ELEMENTS $\left\{ \begin{array}{l} \text{TONIC SOUNDS.} \\ \text{ASPIRATE SOUNDS.} \\ \text{COMBINED SOUNDS.} \end{array} \right.$

TONIC SOUNDS *are those produced by the voice.*

ASPIRATE SOUNDS *are those produced by the breath.*

COMBINED SOUNDS are those produced by both voice and breath.

Phonic Chart.

Tonic Sounds.

1. ā as in lāke, māte.	11. ĭ as in ĭt, sĭt.
2. ă as in măt, răt.	12. ō as in sō, ōld.
3. ä as in bär, fär.	13. ŏ as in nŏt, bŏx.
4. ạ as in ball, fall.	14. ū as in ūse, mūse.
5. â as in fâre, câre.	15. ŭ as in ŭp, nŭt.
6. à as in àsk, tàsk.	16. û as in fûr, cûr.
7. ē as in ēve, hē.	17. o͞o as in to͞o, o͞oze.
8. ĕ as in ĕnd, lĕt.	18. o͝o as in bo͝ok, lo͝ok.
9. ẽ as in ẽarn, hẽr.	19. oi as in oil, moist.
10. ī as in īce, īle.	20. ou as in out, scout.

Aspirate Sounds.

1. k as in kid, kite.	6. t as in ten, tent.
2. f as in fur, first.	7. ch as in chat, chin.
3. p as in pint, pay.	8. sh as in she, shay.
4. h as in her, hit.	9. wh as in when, whit.
5. s as in sat, sin.	10. th as in thin, thick.

Combined Sounds.

1. r as in rare, rain.	8. th as in they, this.
2. n as in nay, nine.	9. z as in azure, azule.
3. l as in lay, line.	10. b as in bay, boy.
4. m as in may, mine.	11. d as in day, dine.
5. g as in gag, gang.	12. v as in vane, vase.
6. j as jay, joint.	13. w as in way, wine.
7. ng as in long, song.	14. y as in yea, yet.

15. z as in zone, zion.

EQUIVALENTS.

Vowels.

ą like ŏ as in whąt.
è like â as in whêre.
e̱ like ā as in the̱y.
ē̱ like û as in hē̱r.
ọ like ōo as in tọ.
į like û as in gįrl.

ò like ŭ as in còme.
ô like ą as in fôr.
ų like ŏŏ as in pųt.
ȳ like ī as in bȳ.
y̆ like ĭ as in kĭtty.
ew like ū as in new.

Consonants.

ç like s as in rāçe.
ꞔ like k as in ꞔăt.
ġ like j as in ꞔāġe.

ṉ like ng as in thiṉk.
s̲ like z as in has̲.
x like ks as in box.

LETTERS

Are characters used to represent or modify sounds.

LETTERS $\begin{cases} \text{VOWELS.} \\ \text{CONSONANTS.} \end{cases}$

VOWELS *are letters which stand for the open sounds of the human voice.* They give audibility.

A DIPHTHONG *is the union of two vowels in one syllable; as,* ou, *in* house.

A DIGRAPH *is the union of two vowels in one syllable, one of which is silent; as,* oa, *in* toast.

A TRIPHTHONG *is the union of three vowels in one syllable; as,* ieu, *in* adieu.

CONSONANTS *are the letters which stand for the sounds made by the obstructed voice and the obstructed breath.* They produce discrimination.

DENTALS *are the letters whose sounds are chiefly formed by the teeth.* They are *s, z, j, ch* and *sh.*

LINGUALS *are the letters whose sounds are chiefly formed by the tongue.* They are *d*, *l*, *r*, and *t*.

PALATALS *are the letters whose sounds are chiefly formed by the palate.* They are *g* and *k*.

LABIALS *are the letters whose sounds are chiefly formed by the lips.* They are *p*, *b*, *w* and *wh*.

F, and *v* are labia-dentals ; *m* is a nasal-labial ; *th* is a lingua-palatal ; *n* is a nasal Lingual ; *ng* is a nasal-palatal.

COGNATES *are the letters whose sounds are produced by the same organs of speech;* thus *k* is a cognate of *g*, and *f* of *v*.

EQUIVALENTS *are letters, or combinations of letters, that represent the same element or sound. I* is an equivalent of *e* in mach*i*ne.

ERRORS IN ARTICULATION.

1. *Omission of one or more elements.*

wīl's	for	wīlds.	stạm	for	storm.
fiel's	for	fields.	wạm	for	warm.
fac's	for	facts.	hist'ry	for	histo ry.
an'	for	and.	nov'l	for	nov ĕl.
frien's	for	friends.	trav'l	for	trav ĕl.
sof'ly	for	soft ly.	chick'n	for	chick ĕn.
blin'ness	for	blind ness.	boist'rous	for	bois têr ous.

2. *Uttering one or more elements that should not be sounded.*

ēv ĕn	for	ev 'n.	sev ĕn	for	sev 'n.
rav ĕl	for	rav 'l.	heav ĕn	for	heav 'n.
tāk ĕn	for	tāk 'n.	soft ĕn	for	sof 'n.
sick ĕn	for	sick 'n.	shak ĕn	for	shak 'n.
driv ĕl	for	driv 'l.	shov ĕl	for	shov 'l.
grov ĕl	for	grov 'l.	shriv ĕl	for	shriv 'l.

3. Substituting one element for another.

ăsk	for	ásk.	re pärt	for re pōrt.
sĕt	for	sĭt.	trŏf fy	for trō phy.
păst	for	pást.	pā rent	for pâr ent.
srill	for	shrill.	bŭn net	for bŏn net.
wirl	for	whirl.	mel ler	for mel lōw.
căre	for	câre.	wis per	for whis per.
shĕt	for	shŭt.	sing in	for sing ing.
sĕnce	for	sĭnce.	chil drun	for chil drĕn.
dănce	for	dánce.	mo munt	for mo mĕnt.
grăss	for	gráss.	harm liss	for harm lĕss.
carse	for	cōurse.	kind niss	for kind nĕss.
sŭl ler	for	cĕl lar.	a gän	for a gain, (ă gĕn).
pil ler	for	pil lōw.	a gänst	for a gainst (ă gĕnst)
for gĭt	for	for gĕt.	hĕrth	for hearth (härth).

WORDS.

A word, spoken or written, is one or more sounds or letters used as the sign of an idea.

WORDS ⎰ PRIMITIVE.
⎱ DERIVATIVE.
⎱ SIMPLE.
⎰ COMPOUND.

A PRIMITIVE WORD *is one which is not derived, but constitutes a root for the formation of other words;* as, man, faith.

A DERIVATIVE WORD *is composed of a primitive and an affix or suffix;* as, man*ly*, faith*ful*.

A SIMPLE WORD *is one that cannot be divided without injuring the sense;* as, boy, book.

A COMPOUND WORD *is a word made up of two or more words;* as, ink-stand, book-binder.

SYLLABICATION.

A SYLLABLE *is a word, or part of a word, uttered by a single act of the voice.*

$$\text{SYLLABLES} \begin{cases} \text{MONOSYLLABLES.} \\ \text{DISSYLLABLES.} \\ \text{TRISSYLLABLES.} \\ \text{POLYSYLLABLES.} \end{cases}$$

A MONOSYLLABLE *is a word of one syllable;* as, *man.*

A DISSYLLABLE *is a word of two syllables;* as, *man*-ly.

A TRISSYLLABLE *is a word of three syllables;* as, *am-i-ty.*

A POLYSLLABLE *is a word of three or more syllables;* as, com-*mend*-a-ble.

THE ULTIMATE *is the last syllable of a word;* as, *ly*, in man-*ly.*

THE PENULT *is the last syllable but one of a word;* as, *nes*, in am-*nes*-ty.

THE ANTEPENULT *is the last syllable but two of a word;* as, *ta*, in spon-*ta*-ne-ous.

THE PREANTEPENULT *is the last syllable but three of a word;* as, *cab*, in vo-*cab*-u-la-ry.

ACCENT

Is the special force given to one or more syllables of a word.

$$\text{ACCENT} \begin{cases} \text{PRIMARY.} \\ \text{SECONDARY.} \end{cases}$$

When two syllables are accented in a word,

THE PRIMARY ACCENT *represents the more forcible.*

THE SECONDARY ACCENT *represents the less forcible.*

The Mark of Acute Accent (') *is used,*

1. *To indicate primary accent;*
2. *To indicate rising inflection.*

The Mark of Grave Accent (`) is used,

1. *To indicate Secondary accent;*
2. *To indicate the falling inflection.*

Exercises in Accent.

1. Vèrácity first of all, and fòrevér.
2. Hunting mèn, not beásts, shall be his game.
3. That blessèd and belovèd child loves evèry wingèd thing.
4. Note the mark of *ac'cent*, and *accent'* the right syllable.
5. Did he *abstract'* an *ab'stract* of your speech from the desk?
6. Earnest prayer is an *in'cense* that can never *incense'* Deity.
7. While you *converse'* with each other, I hold *con'verse* with nature.
8. Unless the *con'vert* be zealous, he will never *convict'* the *con'vict* of his errors, and *convert'* him.
9. If the *pro'test* of the minority be not expected, they will *protest'* against your notes.
10. If the farmer *produce' prod'uce* enough for his family, he will not *transfer'* his title to that estate, though the *trans'fer* is legal.

Exercises in Articulation.

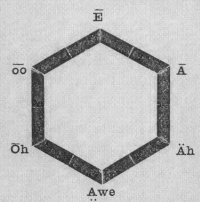

Explanation. Utter all the sounds indicated by the letters on the corners of the Hexagon until great ease and good articulation is acquired.

EXAMPLES.

In the following exercises an erect position of body should be maintained, the head should be held up, the shoulders thrown back, and the chest should be kept full.

The silent letters are omitted in some of the examples, and the words are marked and spelled as they should be pronounced.

Students should read the sentences separately and in concert, uttering all the sounds with force and distinctness. The student should also, be required to analyze every word.

1. Thŭ bōld, băd baĭz brōk bōlts ănd bärz.

2. Hī ŏn ă hĭl Hū hĕrd harsĕz harnĭ hofs.

3. Chárj thē ōld măn to choz ă chaĭs chēz.

4. A thousănd shrēks far hōplĕs mērsĭ kal.

5. Now sĕt thŭ tēth ănd strĕtch thŭ nŏstrĭls wĭde.

6. Hē wŏcht ănd wĕpt, hē fĕlt ănd prād far all.

7. A bĭg blăk bŭg bĭt ă bĭg blăk bâr.

8. Āt grāt grā gēs grāzĭng gāly ĭnto Grēs.

9.

The whales whirled and whirled, and bared their broad brown backs.

10.

The strife ceaseth, peace approacheth, and the good man rejoiceth.

11.

Amos Ames, the amiable aeronaut, aided in an aerial voyage at the age of eighty-eight.

12.

Sheba Sherman Shelly sharpened his shears and sheared his seventeen hundred and seventeen sheep.

13.

Benjamin Bramble Blimber, a blundering baker, borrowed the banker's birchen broom to brush the blinding cobwebs from his brain.

14.

What whim led White Whitney to whittle, whistle, whisper, and whimper near the wharf, where a floundering whale might wheel and whirl?

15.

Thirty-three thousand and thirty-three thoughtless youths thronged the thoroughfare, and thought that they could thwart three thousand thieves by throwing thimbles at them.

16.

Amidst the mists and coldest frosts,
With stoutest wrists, and loudest boasts,
He thrusts his fists against the posts
And still insists he sees the ghosts.

17.

A storm ariseth on the sea. A model vessel is struggling amidst the war of elements, quivering and shivering, shrinking and battling like a thinking being. The merciless, racking whirlwinds, like frightful fiends, howl and moan, and send sharp, shrill shrieks through the creaking cordage, snapping the sheets and masts. The sturdy sailors stand to their tasks, and weather the severest storm of the sea.

18.

Theophilus Thistle, the successful thistle sifter, in sifting a sieve full of unsifted thistles, thrust three thousand thistles through the thick of his thumb; see that thou, in sifting a sieve full of unsifted thistles, thrust not three thousand thistles through the thick of thy thumb. Success to the successful thistle sifter!

19. THE BOOT BLACKS.

A day or two ago, during a lull in business, two little bootblacks, one white and one black, were standing at the corners doing nothing, when the white bootblack agreed to black the black bootblack's boots. The black bootblack was, of course, willing to have his boots blacked by his fellow bootblack, and the bootblack who had agreed to black the black bootblack's boots went to work.

When the bootblack had blacked one of the black bootblack's boots till it shone in a manner that would make any bootblack proud, this bootblack who had agreed to black the black bootblack's boots refused to black the other boot of the black bootblack until the black bootblack, who had consented to have the white bootblack black his boots should add five cents to the amount the white bootblack had made blacking other men's boots. This the bootblack whose boot had been blacked refused to do, saying it was good enough for a black bootblack to have one boot blacked, and he didn't care whether the boot that the white bootblack hadn't blacked was blacked or not.

This made the bootblack who had blacked the black bootblack's boot as angry as a bootblack often gets, and he vented his black wrath by spitting upon the blacked boot of the black bootblack. This raised the latent passions of the black bootblack, and he proceeded to boot the white bootblack with the boot which the white bootblack had blacked. A fight ensued, in which the white bootblack who had refused to black the unblacked boot of the black bootblack blacked the black bootblack's visionary organ, and in which the black bootblack wore all the blacking off his blacked boot in booting the white bootblack.

20. SAMUEL SHORT'S SUCCESS.

Shrewd Simon Short sewed shoes. Seventeen summers' speeding storms, succeeding sunshine, successively saw Simon's small shabby shop standing staunch, saw Simon's selfsame sign still swinging, silently specifying: "SIMON SHORT, SMITFIELD'S SOLE SURVIVING SHOEMAKER. SHOES SEWED, SOLED SUPERFINELY."

Simon's spry, sedulous spouse, Sally Short, sewed shirts, stitched sheets, stuffed sofas. Simon's six stout sturdy sons,—Seth, Samuel,

Stephen, Saul, Shadrach, Silas, sold sundries. Sober Seth sold sugar, starch, spices; Simple Sam sold saddles, stirrups, screws; Sagacious Stephen sold silks, satins, shawls; Skeptical Saul sold silver salvers, silver spoons; Selfish Shadrach sold shoestrings, soaps, saws, skates; Slack Silas sold Sally Short's stuffed sofas.

Some seven summers since, Simon's second son, Samuel, saw Sophia Sophronia Spriggs somewhere. Sweet, sensible, smart, Sophia Sophronia Spriggs. Sam soon showed strange symptoms. Sam seldom stayed storing, selling saddles. Sam sighed sorrowfully, sought Sophia Sophronia's society, sang several serenades slily. Simon stormed, scolded severely, said Sam seemed so silly, singing such shameful, senseless songs.

"Strange Sam should slight such splendid summer sales," said Simon. "Strutting spend-thrift! Scatter-brained simpleton!"

"Softly, softly, sire," said Sally, "Sam's smitten—Sam's spied sweetheart."

"Sentimental schoolboy!" snarled Simon; "Smitten! Stop such stuff!"

Simon sent Sally's snuff-box spinning, seized Sally's scissors, smashed Sally's spectacles, scattering several spools.

"Snarling scoundrel! Sam's shocking silence shall surcease!" Scowling Simon stopped speaking, starting swiftly shopward. Sally sighed sadly. Summoning Sam she spoke sweet sympathy.

"Sam," said she, "sire seems singularly snappish; so sonny, stop strolling sidewalks, stop smoking segars, spending specia superfluously; stop sprucing so; stop singing serenades—stop short; sell saddles, sonny; sell saddles sensibly; see Sophia Sophronia Spriggs soon; she's sprightly, she's staple, so solicit, sure; so secure Sophia speedily, Sam."

"So soon; so soon?" said Sam, standing stock still. "So soon! surely," said Sally, smiling, specially since sire shows such spirit."

So Sam somewhat scared, sauntered slowly, shaking stupendously.

Sam soliloquizes: "Sophia Sophronia Spriggs Short—Sophia Sophronia Sprigs Short—Sophia Sophronia Short, Samuel Short's spouse—sounds splendid! Suppose she should say, she shan't?"

Soon Sam spied Sophia starching shirts, singing softly. Seeing Sam she stopped starching; saluted Sam smilingly; Sam stammered shockingly.

"Sp-sp-splendid summer season, Sophia."

"Somewhat sultry," suggested Sophia.

"Sar-sartin, Sophia," said Sam. (*Silence seventeen seconds.*)

"Selling saddles still, Sam?"

"Sar-sar-sartin," said Sam, starting suddenly.

"Season's somewhat soporific," said Sam steadily staunching streaming sweat, shaking sensibly.

"Sartin," said Sophia, smiling significantly.

"Sip some sweet sherbet, Sam." (*Silence sixty seconds.*)

"Sire shot sixty sheldrakes, Saturday," said Sophia.

"Sixty? sho!" said Sam. (*Silence seventy-seven seconds.*)

"See sister Susan's sunflowers," said Sophia, sociably scattering such stiff silence.

Sophia's sprightly sauciness stimulated Sam strangely; so Sam suddenly spoke sentimentally: "Sophia, Susan's sunflowers seem saying, Samuel Short, Sophia Sophronia Spriggs, stroll serenely, seek some sequestered spot, some sylvan shade. Sparkling spring shall sing soul-stirring strains; sweet songsters shall silence secret sighing; super-angelic sylphs shall"—

Sophia snickered: so Sam stopped.

"Sophia," said Sam, solémnly.

"Sam," said Sophia.

"Sophia, stop smiling. Sam Short's sincere. Sam's seeking some sweet spouse, Sophia."

"Speak, Sophia, speak! Such suspense speculates sorrow."

"Seek sire, Sam; seek sire."

So Sam sought sire Spriggs. Sire Spriggs said, "*Sartin.*"

INTONATION

Is the act of varying the voice so as to best convey the thought.

$$\text{INTONATION} \begin{cases} 1. & \text{QUALITY.} \\ 2. & \text{MELODY.} \\ 3. & \text{FORM.} \\ 4. & \text{FORCE.} \\ 5. & \text{TIME.} \\ 6. & \text{STRESS.} \end{cases}$$

QUALITY

Is the kind of voice.

$$\text{QUALITY} \begin{cases} 1. & \text{PURE.} \\ 2. & \text{IMPURE.} \end{cases}$$

THE PURE QUALITY

Is that used in all pure and chaste expressions.

$$\text{PURE QUALITY} \begin{cases} 1. & \text{SIMPLE PURE.} \\ 2. & \text{OROTUND.} \end{cases}$$

THE SIMPLE PURE

Is that used in common address.

How Produced. {
1. Raise the Larnyx.
2. Lower the Soft Palate.
3. Place tongue in natural position.
4. Direct breath to front of the mouth.
}

EXAMPLES.

1. This tragical tale, which, they say, is a true one,
Is old; but the manner is wholly a new one.
One *Ovid*, a writer of some reputation,
Has told it before in a tedious narration;
In a style, to be sure, of remarkable fulness,
But which nobody reads on account of its dulness.

2. "Gentlemen and ladies," said the showman, "here you have a magnificent painting of Daniel in the lion's den. Daniel can be easily distinguished from the lions by the green cotton umbrella under his arm."

3. And he said, A certain man had two sons; and the younger of them said to his father, Father, give me the portion of goods that falleth to me. And he divided unto them his living.

THE OROTUND

Is an open, round tone employed in the expression of grand, lofty, and sublime thoughts.

How Produced. {
1. Depress the Larnyx.
2. Raise the Soft Palate.
3. Drop back the tongue.
4. Direct breath vertically.
}

EXAMPLES.

1. By Nebo's lonely mountain,
    On this side Jordan's wave,
    In a vale in the land of Moab,
    There lies a lonely grave;
    But no man dug that Sepulchre,
    And no man saw it e'er,
    For the angel of God upturned the sod
    And laid the dead man there.

2. Bless the Lord, O my soul! O Lord, my God, thou art very great; thou art clothed with honor and majesty; who coverest thyself with light as with a garment; who stretchest out the heavens like a curtain; who layeth the beams of his chambers in the waters; who maketh the clouds his chariot; who walketh upon the wings of the wind; who maketh his angels spirits, his ministers a flaming fire; who laid the foundations of the earth, that it should not be removed forever.

THE IMPURE QUALITY

Is that employed in evil emotions.

IMPURE QUALITY
{
1. ASPIRATE.
2. PECTORAL.
3. GUTTURAL.
4. FALSETTO.
}

THE ASPIRATE

Is the whisper, which may or may not possess vocality.

ASPIRATE
{
1. PURE.
2. VOCAL.
}

THE PURE ASPIRATE

Is the Aspirate having no vocality.

EXAMPLES.

1. While thronged the citizens with terror dumb,
   Or whispered with white lips, "The foe!
      They come! they come!"

2. Soldiers! you are now within a few steps of the enemies' outposts. Our scouts report them as slumbering in parties around their watchfires and utterly unprepared for our approach. A swift and noiseless advance around that projecting rock and we are upon them. We'll capture them without the possibility of resistance. Forward!

THE VOCAL ASPIRATE

Is the Aspirate partly vocalized.

EXAMPLES.

1. All heaven and earth are still, though not in sleep,
   But breathless, as we grow when feeling most,
   And silent, as we stand in thoughts too deep;
      All heaven and earth are still; from the high host
      Of stars to the lulled lake and mountain coast,
      All is concentrated in a life intense.

2. I see the smoke of the furnaces where manacles and fetters are still forged for human limbs. I see the visages of those who by stealth and at midnight labor in this work of hell, foul and dark, as may become the artificers of such instruments of misery and torture.

THE PECTORAL

Is the round, deep, throat tone indicative of grief, anger and solemnity.

EXAMPLES.

1. They're gone, they're gone! the glimmering spark hath fled!
   The wife and child are numbered with the dead.
   On the cold hearth outstretched in solemn rest,
   The babe lay frozen on its mother's breast:
   The gambler came at last—but all was o'er—
   Dread silence reigned around:—the clock struck four!

2. Of old Thou hast laid the foundation of the earth; and the heavens are the work of thy hands. They shall perish, but thou shalt endure; yea, all of them shalt wax old like a garment; as a vesture shalt thou change them, and they shall be changed; but thou art the same; and thy years shall have no end.

THE GUTTURAL

Is the rough, throat tone indicative of contempt, malice and settled hate.

EXAMPLES.

1. I loathe ye in my bosom,
   I scorn ye with mine eye,
   And I'll taunt ye with my latest breath,
   And fight ye till I die!
   I ne'er will ask ye quarter,
   And I ne'er will be your slave;
   But I'll swim the sea of slaughter
   Till I sink beneath its wave!

2. And it came to pass at noon, that Elijah mocked them, and said, Cry aloud; for he is a God: either he is talking, or he is pursuing, or he is in a journey, or peradventure he sleepeth, and must be awaked.

THE FALSETTO

Is a piercing elevated tone expressive of pain, fear or distress.

EXAMPLES.

1. Back, ruffians, back! nor dare to tread
   Too near the body of my dead;
   Nor touch the living boy; I stand
   Between him and your lawless band.
   Take *me*, and bind these arms—these hands,—
   With Russia's heaviest iron bands,
   And drag me to Siberia's wild
   To perish if 'twill save my child!

2. Yes, it is worth talking of! But that's how you always try to put me down. You fly into a rage, and then, if I only try to speak, you wont hear me. That's how you men will always have all the talk to yourselves.

MELODY,

In Elocution, is the succession of vocal sounds.

MELODY
1. PITCH.
2. INFLECTION.
3. CADENCE.

PITCH

Is the descent or ascent of tone.

$$\text{PITCH} \begin{cases} \text{1. NATURAL.} \\ \text{2. LOW.} \\ \text{3. HIGH.} \end{cases}$$

NATURAL PITCH

Is the ordinary descent or ascent of tone.

EXAMPLES.

1. There's a burden of grief on the breezes of spring,
    And a song of regret from the bird on its wing;
    There's a pall on the sunshine and over the flowers,
    And a shadow of graves on these spirits of ours;
    For a star hath gone down from the night of our sky,
    On whose brightness we gazed as the war cloud rolled by;
    So tranquil and steady and clear were its beams,
    That they fell like a vision of peace on our dreams.

2. The maxim that no people ought to be free till they are fit to use their freedom, is worthy of the fool in the old story, who resolved not to go into the water till he had learned to swim. If men are to wait for liberty till they become wise and good in slavery, they may indeed wait forever.

LOW PITCH

Is a descent of tone below the Natural.

It is employed in reverence, sublimity and grandeur.

EXAMPLES.

1. So live that when thy summons comes to join
    The innumerable caravan that moves
    To that mysterious realm, where each shall take
    His chamber in the silent halls of death,
    Thou go not like the quarry-slave at night

Scourged to his dungeon, but sustained and soothed
By an unfaltering trust, approach thy grave
Like one who wraps the drapery of his couch
About him, and lies down to pleasant dreams.

2. But, whatever may be our fate, be assured, be assured that this declaration will stand. It may cost treasures, and it may cost blood, but it will stand, and it will richly compensate for both.

HIGH PITCH

Is an ascent of tone above the Natural.

It is employed in joyous or impassioned speech.

EXAMPLES.

1. Cry Holiday! Holiday! let us be gay,
   And share in the rapture of heaven and earth;
   For see what a sunshiny joy they display,
   To welcome the Spring on the day of her birth;
   While the elements, gladly outpouring their voice,
   Nature's paean proclaim, and in chorus rejoice!

2. It is in vain to extenuate the matter. Gentlemen may cry, peace, peace! but there is no peace. The war has actually begun. The next gale that sweeps from the north will bring to our ears the clash of resounding arms! Our brethren are already in the field! Why stand we here idle? Is life so dear, or peace so sweet, as to be purchased at the price of chains and slavery? Forbid it Almighty God! I know not what course others may take, but as for me, give me liberty or give me death!!

INFLECTION

Is the bend of the voice.

$$\text{INFLECTION} \begin{cases} 1. \text{ RISING.} \\ 2. \text{ FALLING.} \\ 3. \text{ COMBINED.} \end{cases}$$

THE RISING INFLECTION

Is the upward movement of the voice.

It is used in uncertainty.

EXAMPLES.

1. 'Twas the night before Christmas, when all through the house
    Not a creature was stirring, not even a mouse,
    Mamma in her kerchief, and I in my cap,
    Had just settled our brain for a long winter's nap,
    When out on the lawn there rose such a clatter—
    I sprang from my bed to see what was the matter.

2. Who covered the earth with such a pleasing variety of fruits
and flowers? Who gave them their delightful fragrance, and painted
them with such exquisite colors? Who caused the same water to
whiten in the lily and blush in the rose! Do not these things prove
the existence of a power infinitely superior to that of any finite being?

THE FALLING INFLECTION

Is the downward movement of the voice.

It is used in certainty.

EXAMPLES.

1. To them his heart, his love, his griefs were given,
    But all his serious thoughts had rest in heaven.
    As some tall cliff that lifts its awful form,
    Swells from the vale, and midway leaves the storm;
    Though 'round its breast the willing clouds are spread,
    Eternal sunshine settles on its head.

2. If ye are beasts, then stand here like fat oxen, waiting for the
butcher's knife! If ye are men,—follow me! Strike down your
guard, gain the mountain passes, and there do bloody work, as did
your sires at old Thermopylæ.

THE COMBINED INFLECTION

Is the upward and downward movement of the voice combined.

It is employed to denote surprise, sarcasm and irony.

1. Now in building of chaises, I tell you what,
   There is always somewhere a weakest spot,
   A chaise breaks down, but does'nt wear out.

2. O Rome! Rome! thou hast been a tender nurse to me. Ay! thou hast given to that poor, gentle, timid shepherd-lad who never knew a hoarser tone than a flute note, muscles of iron and a heart of flint, taught him to drive the sword through plaited mail and links of rugged brass, and warm it in the marrow of his foe:—to gaze into the glaring eyeballs of the fierce Numidian lion even as a boy upon a laughing girl.

CADENCE

Is the tone used in closing a sentence.

It is impossible to give rules which would be a safe guide in regulating the tone and movement of the voice so as to have a correct cadence.

1. Practice counting, one, two, three, four, five etc.

2. *How to practice sentence below.*
   {
   1. Read it naturally.
   2. "   " with Rising Inflection.
   3. "   "   "   Falling Inflection.
   4. "   "   "   Combined Inflection.
   }

   When the winds and the waves lie together asleep,
   The moon and the fairies are watching the deep.

FORM

Is the manner of emitting tone (voice).

$$\text{FORM} \begin{cases} 1. & \text{NATURAL.} \\ 2. & \text{EFFUSIVE.} \\ 3. & \text{EXPULSIVE.} \\ 4. & \text{EXPLOSIVE.} \end{cases}$$

NATURAL FORM

Is that used in ordinary address.

EXAMPLES.

1. Have you ever heard of the wonderful one-*hoss*-shay,
   That was built in such a logical way
   It ran a hundred years to a day,
   And then, of a sudden, it—ah, but stay,
   I'll tell you what happened without delay:

2. Well, sir, he had the biggest, catty-cornedest pianner you ever laid your eyes on; somethin like a distracted billiard table on three legs. The lid was histed, and mighty well it was. If it hadn't been he'd a tore the inside clean out, and scattered em to the four winds of heaven.

EFFUSIVE FORM

Is a gentle tone usually employing the swell.

It expresses beauty, pathos and mildness.

EXAMPLES.

1. We shall all go home to our Father's house—
   To our Father's house in the skies
   Where the hope of our souls shall have no blight,
   And our love no broken ties;

We shall roam on the banks of the river of peace,
  And bathe in its blissful tide;
And one of the joys of that heaven will be
  The little boy that died.

2. Like as a father pitieth his children, so the Lord pitieth them that fear him. For he knoweth our frame; he remembereth that we are dust. As for man, his days are as grass; as a flower of the field so he flourisheth; For the wind passeth over it, and it is gone; and the place thereof shall know it no more.

EXPULSIVE FORM

Is a heavy tone used in great emotion and determination.

EXAMPLES.

1. Why not reform? That's easily said;
    But I've gone through such wretched treatment,
  Sometimes forgetting the taste of bread,
    And scarce remembering what meat meant,
  That my poor stomach's *past* reform;
    And there are times, when mad with thinking,
  I'd sell out heaven for something warm
    To prop a horrible inward sinking.

2. Sir, the declaration will inspire the people with increased courage. Instead of a long and bloody war for restoration of privileges, for redress of grievances, for chartered immunities, held under a British king, set before them the glorious object of entire independence and it will breathe into them anew the breath of life. Read this declaration at the head of the army; every sword will be drawn from its scabbard, and the solemn vow uttered, to maintain it or perish on the bed of honor. Publish it from the pulpit; Religion will approve

it, and the love of Religious liberty will cling around it, resolved to stand with or fall with it. Send it to the public halls; proclaim it there; let them hear it, who heard the first roar of the enemie's cannon; let them see it who saw their brothers and their sons fall on the field of Bunker Hill and in the streets of Lexington and Concord,— and the very walls will cry out in its support.

EXPLOSIVE FORM

Is a heavy tone employed in command, grand description and impressioned language.

EXAMPLES.

1. I saw the corse, the mangled corse
   And then I cried for vengeance!
   Rouse, ye Romans! rouse ye slaves!
   Have ye brave sons? Look in the next fierce brawl
   To see them die. Have ye fair daughters? Look
   To see them live, torn from your arms, disdained,
   Dishonored; and if ye dare call for justice,
   Be answered by the lash!

2. Were I an American, as I am an Englishman, while a single foreign troop remained in my country, I would never lay down my arms. Never, *Never*, NEVER.

FORCE

Is the degree of power of the voice.

FORCE $\begin{cases} 1. & \text{SUBDUED.} \\ 2. & \text{NATURAL.} \\ 3. & \text{HEAVY.} \end{cases}$

SUBDUED FORCE

Accompanies the Effusive Form.

EXAMPLES.

1. Only waiting till the shadows
      Are a little longer grown;
   Only waiting till the glimmer
      Of the day's last beam is flown;
   Till the night of earth is faded
      From the heart once full of day;
   Till the stars of heaven are breaking
      Through the twilight soft and gray.

2. But while she was still very young,—O very, very young, the sister drooped, and came to be so weak that she could no longer stand in the window at night; and then the child looked sadly out by himself, and when he saw the star, turned round and said to the patient, pale face on the bed:

NATURAL FORCE

Accompanies Natural Form.

EXAMPLES.

1. Noiselessly as the springtime
      Her crown of verdure weaves,
   And all the trees on all the hills
      Open their thousand leaves,
   So, without sound of music,
      Or voice of them that wept,
   Silently down from the mountain crown
      The great procession swept.

2. There are men who get one idea into their heads, and but one, and they make the most of it. You can see it and almost feel it in their presence. On all occasions it is produced, till it is worn as thin as charity. They remind you of a twenty-four pounder discharged at a hummingbird. You hear a tremendous noise, see a volume of smoke, but you look in vain for the effects. The bird is scattered to atoms.

HEAVY FORCE

Accompanies the Expulsive and Explosive Forms.

EXAMPLES.

1. The storm o'er the ocean flew furious and fast,
   And the waves rose in foam at the voice of the blast,
   And heavily labored the gale-beaten ship,
   Like a stout-hearted swimmer, the spray at his lip;
   And dark was the sky o'er the mariner's path,
   Save when the wild lightning illumined in wrath.

2. My brethren, let us no longer live to ourselves. Let us arise and put our hands to the great work in which the nations are now moving. Wondrous things are taking place in the four quarters of the globe. The world is waking up after a long sleep, and is teeming with projects and efforts to extend the empire of truth and happiness. This is the day of which the prophets sung. Let us not sleep, while others are rousing themselves to action. Let every soul come up to the help of the Lord. Let not one be left behind. He that hath absolutely nothing to give, let him pray. Let no one be idle. This is a great day and the Lord requires every hand in the work.

TIME

Is the duration of utterance.

$$\text{TIME} \begin{cases} 1. \text{ QUANTITY.} \\ 2. \text{ RATE.} \\ 3. \text{ PAUSE.} \end{cases}$$

QUANTITY

Is the length of time we dwell on a word.

$$\text{QUANTITY} \begin{cases} 1. \text{ SHORT.} \\ 2. \text{ NATURAL.} \\ 3. \text{ LONG.} \end{cases}$$

SHORT QUANTITY

Consists of a quick utterance.

It is used in *gayety*, *command* and *vile emotions*.

EXAMPLES.

1. Quick! man the life-boat! See yon bark,
   That drives before the blast!
   Ther's a rock ahead, the fog is dark,
   And the storm comes thick and fast.

2. And he answering, said to his father, Lo, these many years do I serve thee, neither transgressed I at any time thy commandments; and yet thou never gavest me a kid, that I might make merry with my friends.

NATURAL QUANTITY

Is that applied to unimpassioned discourse.

EXAMPLES.

1. They've left the school-house, Charlie, where years ago we sat
   And shot our paper bullets at the master's time-worn hat;
   The hook is gone on which it hung, the master sleepeth now
   Where schoolboy tricks can never cast a shadow o'er his brow.

2. There is one accomplishment, in particular, which I would earnestly recommend to you. Cultivate assiduously the ability to read well. Where one person is really interested by music, twenty are pleased by good reading. Where one person is capable of becoming a skillful musician, twenty may become good readers. Where there is one occasion suitable for the exercise of musical talent, there are twenty for that of good reading.

LONG QUANTITY

Consists of a prolonged utterance.

It is used in *Pathos, Entreaty,* and *Sublimity.*

EXAMPLES.

1. O the long and dreary Winter!
   O the cold and cruel Winter!
   Ever thicker, thicker, thicker
   Froze the ice on lake and river;
   Ever deeper, deeper, deeper
   Fell the snow o'er all the landscape,
   Fell the covering snow, and drifted
   Through the forest 'round the village.

2.   To die—to sleep,—
No more! and, by a sleep, to say we end
The heartache, and the thousand natural shocks
That flesh is heir to,—'tis a consummation
Devoutly to be wished. To die,—to sleep;—
To sleep!—perchance to dream—aye, there's the rub!
For, in that sleep of death, what dreams may come,
When we have shuffled off this mortal coil,
Must give us pause!

RATE

Is the velocity of utterance.

$$\text{RATE} \begin{cases} 1. & \text{SLOW.} \\ 2. & \text{NATURAL.} \\ 3. & \text{FAST.} \end{cases}$$

SLOW RATE

Accompanies Long Quantity.

EXAMPLES.

1. O lonely tomb in Moab's land!
   O dark Beth-peor's hill!
Speak to these curious hearts of ours
   And teach them to be still.
God hath His mysteries of grace,—
   Ways that we cannot tell.

2. And the raven, never flitting, still is sitting, still is sitting,
On the pallid bust of Pallas, just above my chamber door;
And his eyes have all the seeming of a demon's that is dreaming,
And the lamplight o'er him streaming, throws his shadow on the
      floor;
And my soul from out that shadow that lies floating on the floor
Shall be lifted—NEVERMORE!

NATURAL RATE

Accompanies Natural Quantity.

EXAMPLES.

1. O good painter, tell me true,
    Has your hand the cunning to draw
    Shapes of things that you never saw?
    Ay? Well, here is an order for you.
   Woods and cornfields a little brown,
    The picture must not be over bright
    Yet all in the golden and gracious light
    Of a cloud when the summer sun is down.

2. To make men patriots, to make men Christians, to make men
the sons of God, let all the doors of heaven be opened, and let God
drop down charmed gifts—winged imaginations, all piercing reason,
and all judging reason. Whatever there is that can make men wiser
and better—let it descend upon the head of him who has consecrated
himself to the work of mankind, and who has made himself an orator
for man's sake and for God's sake.

FAST RATE

Accompanies Short Quantity.

EXAMPLES.

1. "It snows," cries the school-boy; "hurrah!" and his shout
    Is ringing through parlor and hall;
   While swift as the wing of the swallow he's out,
    And his playmates have answered his call.
   It makes the heart leap but to witness their joy;
    Proud wealth has no pleasure, I trow,
   Like the rapture that throbs in the pulse of the boy
    As he gathers his treasures of snow.

2. A cannon which breaks its moorings becomes abruptly some
indescribable, supernatural beast. It is a machine which transforms
itself into a monster. This mass runs on its wheels, like billiard

balls, inclines with the rolling, plunges with the pitching, goes, comes, stops, seems to meditate, resumes it course, shoots from one end of the ship to the other like an arrow, whirls, steals away, evades, prances, strikes, breaks, kills, exterminates.

PAUSE

Is a cessation of voice.

PAUSE { 1. SHORT.
2. NATURAL.
3. LONG.

SHORT PAUSE

Accompanies Short Quantity.

EXAMPLES.

1. I sprang to the stirrup, and Joris and he :
   I galloped, Dirk galloped, we galloped all three ;
   "God speed !" cried the watch as the gate-bolts undrew ;
   "Speed !" echoed the wall to us galloping through.
   Behind shut the postern, the light sank to rest,
   And into the midnight we galloped abreast.

2. John,. be quick. Get some water. Throw the powder over-board. "It cannot be reached." Jump into the boat, then. Shove off. There goes the powder. Thank heaven. We are safe.

NATURAL PAUSE

Accompanies Natural Quantity.

EXAMPLES.

1. There's a land far away, 'mid the stars we are told,
   Where they know not the sorrows of time;
   Where the pure waters wander through valleys of gold,
   And life is a pleasure sublime.

2. Every evil that we conquer is good for our souls. The Sandwich Islander believes that the strength and valor of the enemy he kills, passes into himself. *Spiritually*, it is so with us, for we gain strength from every temptation we resist.

LONG PAUSE

Accompanies Long Quantity.

EXAMPLES.

1. To be, or not to be, that is the question:
   Whether 'tis nobler in the mind to suffer
   The slings and arrows of outrageous fortune;
   Or to take arms against a sea of troubles,
   And by opposing, end them?

2. Pause a moment. I heard a footstep. Listen now. I heard it again; but it is going from us. It sounds fainter,—still fainter. It is gone.

3. Be ye patient! I have but a few more words to say. I am going to my cold and silent grave; my lamp of life is nearly extinguished; my race is run; the grave opens to receive me, and I sink into its bosom! I have but one request to make at my departure from this world,—it is the charity of silence! Let no man write my epitaph; for, as no man who knows my motives dare now vindicate them, let no prejudice or ignorance asperse them. Let them and me repose in obscurity and peace, and my tomb remain uninscribed, until other times and other men can do justice to my character.

STRESS

Is the manner of applying force to a tone.

STRESS $\left\{\begin{array}{l}\text{1. INITIAL.}\\ \text{2. FINAL.}\\ \text{3. MEDIAN.}\\ \text{4. COMPOUND.}\\ \text{5. THOROUGH.}\\ \text{6. INTERMITTENT.}\end{array}\right.$

INITIAL STRESS

Is force on the beginning of a word or syllable.

It accompanies *Lively Narration*, and *Intense Feeling* and *Emotion*.

EXAMPLES.

1. I see it is a trick,
    Got up betwixt you and the woman there.
    I must be taught my *duty* and by you.
    You knew my word was law, and
    Yet you dared to slight it.
    Well—for I will take the boy;
    But *go* you hence, and never see me more.

2. There's a dance of leaves in that aspen bower;
    There's a titter of winds in that beechen tree;
    There's a smile on the fruit, and a smile on the flowers,
    And a laugh from the brook that runs to the sea.

FINAL STRESS

Is force on the last part of a word or syllable.

It accompanies expressions of *Hatred*, *Revenge* and *Contempt*.

EXAMPLES.

1. Ye gods, it doth amaze me!
    A man of such a *feeble* temper should
    So get the start of the *majestic* world,
    And bear the palm *alone*.

2. Sir, before God, I believe the time is come. My judgment approves this measure, and my whole heart is in it. All that I have, and all that I am, and all that I hope in this life, I am now ready here to stake upon it; and I leave off as I began, that, live or die, survive or perish, I am for the declaration.

MEDIAN STRESS

Is that which accompanies Effusive Form.

It is used in *Reverence, Sublimity* and *Devotion*.

EXAMPLES.

1. Leaves have their time to fall,
      And flowers to wither at the North wind's breath,
    And stars to set; but all,
      Thou hast all seasons for thine own, O Death!
    We know when moons shall wane,
      When summer birds from far shall cross the sea,
    When Autumn's hue shall tinge the golden grain;
      But who shall teach us when to look for thee?

2. O thou that rollest above, round as the shield of my fathers! whence are thy beams, O sun! thy everlasting light! Thou comest forth in thy awful beauty, the stars hide themselves in the sky; the moon, cold and pale, sinks into the western wave. But thou thyself movest alone: who can be a companion of thy course?

COMPOUND STRESS

Is the Initial and Final Combined.

It accompanies the *Combined Inflection.*

EXAMPLES.

1. Gone to be married! Gone to swear a peace!
   False blood to false blood joined! Gone to be friends!
   Shall Lewis have Blanche, and Blanche these provinces?
   It is not so; thou hast misspoken, misheard;
   Be well advised, tell o'er thy tale again:
   It cannot be; thou dost but say 'tis so.

2. *I'll* have my *bond;* I will not hear thee speak:
   I'll have my bond; and therefore speak no more.
   I'll not be made a *soft* and dull-eyed *fool,*
   To shake the head, relent, and sigh, and *yield*
   To Christian intercessors.

THOROUGH STRESS

Accompanies Heavy Force.

EXAMPLES.

1. Blaze with your seried columns! I will not bend the knee;
   The shackles ne'er again shall bind the arm which now is free!
   I've mailed it with the thunder when the tempest muttered low,
   And when it falls ye well may dread the lightning of its blow.

I've scared you in the city; I've scalped you on the plain;
Go, count your chosen where they fell beneath my leaden rain!
I scorn your proffered treaty; the pale-face I defy;
Revenge is stamped upon my spear, and "blood" my battle-cry!

2. O liberty! O sound once delightful to every Roman ear! O sacred privilege of Roman citizenship! once sacred, now trampled upon! But what then—is it come to this? Shall an inferior magistrate, a governor, who holds his power of the Roman people, in a Roman province, within sight of Italy, bind, scourge, torture with fire and red-hot plates of iron, and at last put to the infamous death of the cross, a Roman Citizen?

INTERMITTENT STRESS

Is a tremulous force of voice.

It is used in expressing *Fatigue* and *Grief*, and is also employed in imitating the *Voice of Old Age.*

EXAMPLES.

1. My tender wife, sweet soother of my care!
    Struck with sad anguish at the stern decree,
  Fell, ling'ring fell, a victim to despair;
    And left the world to wretchedness and me.
  Pity the sorrows of a poor old man,
    Whose trembling limbs have borne him to your door;
  Whose days are dwindled to the shortest span:
    Oh! give relief and heaven will bless your store.

2. A young mother knelt in the cabin below,
    And pressing her babe to her bosom of snow,
    She prayed to her God, 'mid the hurricane wild,
    "O Father have mercy, look down on my child!"

SLUR

Is that rapid, smooth-gliding, subdued movement of the voice, which is placed on parenthetical clauses.

When the parenthetical clause is placed in the middle of a sentence, it should be preceded and followed by a pause. As the reader passes from the important clause to the slurred clause, or from the slurred to the important clause, the facial expression should change.

EXAMPLES.

1. History, *in a word*, is replete with moral lessons.

2. Every condition of life, *be it what it may*, has both hardships and pains.

3. Thompson, *who was blessed with a strong and copious fancy*, drew his images from nature itself.

4. One truth is clear, *enough for man to know*,
   Virtue alone is happiness below.

5. In parts superior what advantage lies?
   Tell, *for you can*, what is it to be wise?

6. Whatever future advances of science may do for us in the matter, *and I hope they may do much*, I must still say this relation is a mystery.

7. Superintendent Brown has again been doing a very sensible thing, *no uncommon thing for him*, in the way of submitting a revised course of study for high schools.

8. The king issued a proclamation which produced an important change, *although it was not generally thought so at the time*, in the financial condition of the whole kingdom.

9. God bless the man who first invented sleep!
   (So Sancho Panza said, and so say I,)
   And bless him, also, that he did not keep
   The great discovery to himself, by making it
   (As well the lucky fellow might)
   A close monopoly of patent-right.

EMPHASIS

Consists chiefly in an increase of vocal force on one or more words of a sentence.

The tone, look, posture, gesture or movement should correspond in emphasis with the emphasized word or words.

Emphasize the following exercises in a simple, direct and natural manner.

EXAMPLES.

1. He is a *very industrious* man.

2. The *perfection* of art is to *conceal* art.

3. It is useless to *discuss* any theory until we *know what the theory is.*

4. *He* is the greatest man *who does the greatest service to his fellow men.*

5. Any *innocent employment* or *harmless amusement* is better than IDLENESS or EMPTINESS.

6. *Industry* is a virtue that is highly valued *among all people* and *in all nations.*

7. The *wicked* flee when *no man* pursueth; but the *righteous* are *bold* as *lions.*

8. A *day*, an *hour*, of *virtuous liberty* is worth a WHOLE ETERNITY in *bondage.*

9. Let us fight for our *country*, our *whole country*, and NOTHING BUT OUR COUNTRY.

In Address.

1. *If the address is formal, the voice falls.*

2. *If the address is informal, the voice rises.*

In Interrogation.

1. *If the question can be answered by "yes" or "no," the voice rises.*

2. *If the question cannot be answered by "yes" or "no," the voice falls.*

GESTICULATION

Is that part of Expression which is addressed to the eye.

$$\text{GESTICULATION} \begin{cases} 1. & \text{POSITION.} \\ 2. & \text{MOVEMENT.} \end{cases}$$

POSITION

Is the manner in which a person stands or sits.

$$\text{POSITION} \begin{cases} 1. & \text{SPEAKING.} \\ 2. & \text{ACTING.} \\ 3. & \text{SITTING.} \\ 4. & \text{STANDING.} \end{cases}$$

SPEAKING
1. Weight of body supported on one foot.
2. Other foot is placed a little in front @ angle of 45°.
3. Knee in advance slightly bent. (May advance or recede.)
4. Reverse this position by standing on other foot, etc.

ACTING
1. Position of actor should always be natural.
2. Should vary according to the impersonation of character assumed.
3. Position may be changed in any direction.
4. The actor always acts an assumed character.

SITTING
1. Feet as in "speaking," knees bent @ angle of 90°.
2. Chin drawn in, head erect, square to front.
3. Shoulders back, form full height.
4. Hands on lap, 6 inches from body.

STANDING
1. Heels together, toes inclined outward @ angle of 60°.
2. Chin drawn in, shoulders thrown back.
3. Arms hang at side, body to front.
4. Figure to full height, stand on ball of foot.

BOWING
1. Always bend body at hips.
2. Never nod the head.
3. Do not bend body at waist.

READING
1. Book in left hand, three fingers below it.
2. Thumb and little finger above it.
3. Fore arm @ an angle of 45°.

MOVEMENT

Has reference to the change of place.

MOVEMENT
1. FACE.
2. EYES.
3. HEAD.
4. BODY.
5. LEGS AND FEET.
6. HANDS.
7. ARMS.

"The *Face* is the index of the soul."

The *Eyes*
1. Burn in anger.
2. Weep in sorrow.
3. Are raised in prayer.
4. Are vacant in thought.
5. Are downcast in shame.

The *Head*
1. Moves forward in expectation.
2. Thrown forward, shows affirmation.
3. Thrown sidewise, shows negation.
4. Thrown up, shows courage and pride.
5. Thrown down, shows grief and shame.
6. Thrown around, shows dislike or horror.

The *Body*
1. Is held back in pride.
2. Is bent in homage and respect.
3. Is prostrate in great humility.
4. Is stooping forward in compassion.
5. Is held erect in courage and firmness.

The *Legs and Feet*
1. Bound in terror.
2. Stamp in anger and authority.
3. Kneel in prayer and humiliation.
4. Retreat in fear or horror.
5. Advance in expectation and bravery.

The *Hands*
1. Are prone in benediction.
2. Are on the eyes in grief and shame.
3. Are on the breast in appeal to conscience.
4. Are wrung in sorrow and anguish.
5. Are extended in friendship and admiration.
6. Are waved in triumph and delight.
7. Are placed on head in pain and affliction.

HANDS
1. SUPINE (*palm upward*).
2. PRONE (*palm downward*).
3. VERTICAL (*palm outward*).
4. POINTING (*forefinger extended*).
5. CLENCHED (*hand closed*).

The SUPINE HAND *is used in Affirmation.*
The PRONE HAND *is used in Negation.*
The VERTICAL HAND *is used in Limitation.*
The POINTING HAND *is used in pointing to some special thing.*
The CLENCHED HAND *is used in intense feeling.*

ARMS
1. FRONT.
2. OBLIQUE.
3. LATTERAL.
4. BACKWARD.

1. HORIZONTAL.
2. DESCENDING.
3. ASCENDING.

The FRONT GESTURE *refers to something definite, near us.*

The OBLIQUE GESTURE *refers to something indefinite, at a distance.*

The LATTERAL GESTURE *refers to something at great distance, or in contrast.*

The BACKWARD GESTURE *refers to something obscure or distant.*

The HORIZONTAL GESTURE *refers to common description.*

The DESCENDING GESTURE *refers to sentienmts of inferiority.*

The ASCENDING GESTURE *refers to sentiments of superiority.*

General Rules for Gesture.

No. 1. Let the arms move from the shoulders.

No. 2. In forcible expression, let the arms move in straight lines.

No. 3. In graceful expression, let the arms move in curved lines.

No. 4. Paint the Picture.

Exercises in Gesticulation.

Abbreviations.

F = Front.

H = Horizontal.	*O = Oblique.*
A = Ascending.	*L = Latteral.*
D = Descending.	*B = Backward.*

[Practice till Gesture becomes natural.]

One Hand Supine.

F.

H. *Before* him lay his unconquered foe.

H. Whatever impedes his progress shall be *removed*.

A. I appeal to the God of *heaven* to vindicate my cause.

A. Columbia, Columbia, to *glory* arise.

D. The first test of a great man is his *humility*.

D. *Down*, down forty fathoms beneath the blue wave.

D. Thou shalt *lie down* with our fathers.

D. Of all mistakes *none* are so fatal as those incurred by prejudice.

O.

H. Truth, honor and *justice* were his motives.

H. What is *man* that thou art mindful of him.

A. Hope is *above* us beckoning us onward.

A. Fix your eyes on the *prize* of a noble ambition.

L.

H. The breeze of morn wafted *incense* on the air.

H. I freely grant *all* that you demand.

A. *Flag* of the free, heart's hope and home.

A. In all his dreams he bore the trophies of a *conqueror*.

D. Away with such vain *illusions*.

D. The truth of his statement I *deny*.

B.

H. Lift the curtains of the *past* and look for a parallel to this.

H. I gaze upon the silent ocean of the *past*.

A. Then rang their *shouts* of joy.

A. *Away—oh! away*—soars the fearless and free.

D. Then we heard their *fiendish* cries.

D. *Away* with an idea so foreign to virtue.

Both Hands Supine.

F.

H. Listen, I *implore* you to the voice of reason.

H. We have no *concessions* to make, my lord.

A. Ye *crags and peaks*, I'm with you once again.

A. *Hail* thou universal God.

D. All personal ambition he *discarded* for his country's good.

D. O mighty Cæsar! Dost thou *lie so low?*

O.

H. His talents he *deposited* on the altar of his country.

H. *Welcome!* once more to your childhood's home.

A. *Hail!* holy angels of light.

A. *Take* my spirit, all omnipotent, to thee.

D. All my fortune at thy *feet*, I lay.

D. Every personal advantage, he *surrendered*.

L.

H. Proclaim the tidings to *all people*.

H. They yet slept in the wide *abyss* of possibility.

A. *Spirits of Freedom*, awake at the shout.

A. Joy, *joy, forever!* my task is forever done.

D. I utterly *renounce* the truth of such a statement.

D. Nature hears the shock and *hurls* her fabric to the dust.

ONE HAND PRONE.

F.

H. *Peace* be unto thee.

A. O God, *withhold* the plague.

D. *Put down* so base a passion.

O.

H. I beg you to *restrain* your passions.

A. Ye gods, *withhold* your vengeance.

D. Men and brethren, *put down* all malice.

L.

H. Trouble and disease threw gloom *over all* his prospects.

A. The storm *spread* darkness o'er the mountain-top.

D. The hand of affection *shall smooth* the turf o'er thy grave.

Both Hands Prone.

F.

H. May the confidence of the good *rest* on thee.

A. Blessed be the *name* of our God.

D. Lay the sod *gently* on his grave.

O.

H. And let the voice of freedom *rest* on the land.

A. May the blessing of *heaven rest* on you evermore.

D. We were in their sight as *worms of the dust.*

L.

H. For the angel of Death *spread his wings* on the blast.

A. Heaven *opened wide* her ever-during gates.

D. Here let the tumults of passion *forever cease.*

One Hand Vertical.

F.

H. Meet and *repel* the invaders of your land.

A. *Forbid* it, God of heaven.

D. Come no *further* ye thing of evil.

O.

H.   His arm *warded* off the blow.

A.   May heaven *avert* the calamity.

D.   *Push away* the stubborn foe.

L.

H.   *Out of my sight*, ye red men.

A.   *Up* to thy place, holy angels.

D.   *Down* to thy abode, evil spirits.

B.

H.   *Away* delusive phantom.

A.   *Back* to thy place holy angel.

D.   *Back* to thy abode false fugitive.

BOTH HANDS VERTICAL.

F.

H.   *Avaunt !* and quit my sight.

A.   *Hide your faces*, holy angels.

D.   Ye demons *hasten* from my sight.

O.

H.   The gates of death in *sunder* break.

A.   May heavenly *angels defend* thee.

D.   *Come no further*, ye writhing souls.

L.

H.   Let them remain *disunited* forever.

A.   With united hearts, let us *drive back* the invader.

D.   Melt and *sink down* ye spectre doubts.

For further practice in Gesticulation, the following most excellent piece is furnished, which should be committed to memory and practiced until proper gesture becomes natural.

THE AMERICAN FLAG.

By Joseph R. Drake.

1. When Freedom, from her mountain height,
    Unfurled her standard to the air,
  She tore the azure robe of night,
    And set the stars of glory there!
  She mingled with its gorgeous dyes
  The milky baldric of the skies,
  And striped its pure celestial white
  With streakings of the morning light;
  Then, from his mansion in the sun,
  She called her eagle-bearer down,
  And gave into his mighty hand
  The symbol of her chosen land!

2. Majestic monarch of the cloud!
    Who reare'st aloft thy regal form,
  To hear the tempest trumpings loud,
  And see the lightning-lances driven,
    When strive the warriors of the storm,
  And rolls the thunder-drum of heaven!
  Child of the sun! to thee 'tis given
    To guard the banner of the free,
  To hover in the sulphur smoke,
  To ward away the battle-stroke,
  And bid its blendings shine afar,
  Like rainbows on the cloud of war—
    The harbingers of victory!

3. Flag of the brave, thy folds shall fly,
   The sign of hope and triumph high.
   When speaks the signal trumpet tone,
   And the long line comes glimmering on—
   Ere yet the life-blood warm and wet,
   Has dimmed the glistening bayonet—
   Each soldier's eye shall brightly turn
   To where the sky-born glories burn;
   And, as his springing steps advance,
   Catch war and vengeance from the glance!
   And when the cannon-mouthings loud
   Heave in wild wreaths the battle-shroud,
   And gory sabers rise and fall,
   Like shoots of flame on midnight's pall;
   Then shall thy meteor glances glow,
      And cowering foes shall sink beneath
   Each gallant arm that strikes below
      That lovely messenger of death.

4. Flag of the seas! on ocean wave
   Thy stars shall glitter o'er the brave,
   When Death, careering on the gale,
   Sweeps darkly 'round the bellied sail,
   And frighted waves rush wildly back,
   Before the broadside's reeling rack;
   Each dying wanderer of the sea
   Shall look at once to heaven and thee,
   And smile to see thy splendors fly,
   In triumph o'er his closing eye.

5. Flag of the free heart's hope and home,
      By angel hands to valor given!
   Thy stars have lit the welkin dome,
      And all thy hues were born in heaven.
   Forever float that standard sheet!
      Where breathes the foe but falls before us,
   With Freedom's soil beneath our feet,
      And Freedom's banner streaming over us?

DIRECTNESS

Is the plain, simple address that we unconsciously employ when endeavoring to convince.

Use your own direct way of expression, as if the thoughts had just been suggested to your own mind.

EXAMPLES.

1. Young men, Ahoy! the rapids are below you.

2. Treat every man as a gentleman, until he has proven himself otherwise.

3. Give every man thine ear, but few thy voice; Take each man's censure but reserve thy judgment.

4. Fellow citizens, you stand here like giants as you are.

5. I cannot, my lords, I will not join in congratulation on misfortune and disgrace.

6. Friends, Romans, countrymen! lend me your ears. I come to bury Cæsar, not to praise him.

7. This is a case, gentlemen of the jury, in which the plaintiff is a widow; yes, gentlemen of the jury, a widow.

8. Let me tell you, Cassius, you yourself are much condemned to have an itching palm, to sell and mart your offices for gold to undeservers.

9. I profess, sir, in my career hitherto, to have kept steadily in view the prosperity and honor of the whole country, and the preservation of the Federal Union.

10. My brave associates, partners of my toil, my feelings, and my fame, can Rolla's words add vigor to the virtuous energies that now inspire your hearts?

EXPRESSION

Is the utterance of thought or feeling with such force as to convey it in the clearest and most pleasing manner.

It is most necessary, to employ correct expression, to feel that which you wish to express,—to have clear ideas concerning what you read or speak. Dr. H. W. Beecher says on this subject, "Fill yourself chock full of the subject; then pull out the bung, and let nature caper."

The student should not try to imitate the expression of others, but use his own natural style.

"To paint the passion's force, and paint it well
The proper action nature's self will tell."

EXAMPLE.

Henry says he will start to Springfield next Monday.

[Practice the above sentence as directed below.]

1. Place emphasis on Henry as if answering question, "Who says etc."
2. Emphasize successively every word in the sentence.
3. Give it every variety of affirmation, negation, and interrogation.
4. Give it as if speaking to a person at a distance.
5. Give it in a pleasant tone and manner.
6. Give it in a sullen tone and manner.
7. Give it in a careless sleepy tone and manner.
8. Give it in an excited tone and manner.
9. Give it in an ironical tone and manner.
10. Give it in a respectful tone and manner.
11. Give it in a serious tone and manner.
12. Give it in a merry tone and manner.

NOTE. The Facial Expression and action should correspond with the tone of voice.

ANTITHESIS

Is the placing of words in contrast to heighten their effect.

There should be a pause after the antithetic words, in nearly all cases.

EXAMPLES.

1. The righteous shall enter into everlasting joy, but the wicked into everlasting punishment.

2. I do not tremble when I meet
   The stoutest of my foes;
   But heaven defend me from the friend
   Who comes and never goes.

3. The cottage was a thatched one,
   The outside old and mean,
   But all within that little cot
   Was wondrous neat and clean.

4. A liar begins by making a falsehood appear like truth, and ends by making a truth appear like falsehood.

5. The world will little note, nor long remember, what we say here; but it can never forget what they did here.

6. If the blaze of Dryden's fire is brighter, the heat of Pope's is more regular and constant. Dryden often surpasses expectation, and Pope never falls below it.

EXCLAMATION

Is the words employed to express strong emotion, feeling or passion.

1. Hence! home, ye idle creatures—get ye gone!

2. Hush!—Hark!—a deep sound strikes like a rising knell.

3. Praise ye the Lord! The Lord's name be praised!

4. Now for the fight! forward through blood and smoke!
5. Clarence has come! false! fleeting! perjured Clarence!
6. Great heaven! how frail thy creature man is made!
How by himself insensibly betrayed!
7. They're gone! they're gone! the glimmering spark hath fled,
The wife and child are numbered with the dead!
8. It is my living sentiment, and, by the blessing of God, it shall be my dying sentiment!—independence now, and independence for-ever!!

EMPHATIC REPETITION

Is the increased expression of repeated words.

EXAMPLES.

1. *Arm*, warriors! ARM for the fight!
2. *Down!* DOWN! cries Mar, your lances DOWN!
3. You *can not*, my Lords, you CAN NOT conquer America.
4. *To arms!* THEY COME! *the Greek!* THE GREEK!
5. This long line passes in solemn array, and lifting up its face to God, cries out, *avenge!* AVENGE!! AVENGE!!!
6. If I were an *American*, as I am an *Englishman*, while a foreign troop remained in my country, I *never* would lay down my arms— *never*, NEVER, NEVER.

IRONY

Is the pronouncing of words in such a manner as to convey a mean-ing directly opposite to that implied by the language.

Irony may vary in expression from the just perceptible tone to the tone of intense bitterness.

1. Your consul's merciful—for this all thanks:
He dares not touch a hair of Catiline!

2. O masters! if I were disposed to stir
   Your hearts and minds to mutiny and rage,
   I should do Brutus wrong, and Cassius wrong;
   Who, you all know, are honorable men.
   I will not do them wrong; I rather choose
   To wrong the dead, to wrong myself, and you,
   Than I will wrong such honorable men.

3. They boast they come but to improve our state, enlarge our thoughts, and free us from the yoke of error! Yes, they will give enlightened freedom to our minds, who are themselves the slaves of passion, avarice and pride. Yes, they offer us their protection as vultures give to lambs—covering and devouring them.

4. "But, Mr. Speaker, we have a right to tax America." Oh, wonderful, transcendent right! the assertion of which has cost this country thirteen provinces, six islands, one hundred thousand lives; and seventy millions of money. Oh, invaluable right! for the sake of which we have sacrificed our right among nations, our importance abroad, and our happiness at home! Oh, right! more dear to us than our existence! which has already cost us so much, and which seems likely to cost us our all.

APOSTROPHE

Is a turning away from a real auditor or audience and addressing an absent or imaginary one.

Practice as if the object or thing addressed were a person.

EXAMPLES.

1. O happiness! our being's end and aim,
   Good, pleasure, ease, content—whate'er thy name;
   That something still which prompts the eternal sigh,
   For which we fear to live and dare to die;
   Which still so near us, yet beyond us lies;
   O'erlook'd, seen double, by the fool and wise;

Plant of celestial seed! if dropp'd below,
Say in what mortal soil thou deign'st to grow?

2. Roll on, thou dark and deep blue ocean, roll!
Ten thousand fleets sweep over thee in vain.
Man marks the earth with ruin—his control
Stops with the shore; upon the watery plain
The wrecks are all thy deed, nor doth remain
A shadow of men's ravage, save his own,
When, for a moment, like a drop of rain,
He sinks into thy depths with bubbling groan,
Without a grave, unknell'd, uncoffin'd and unknown.

INTERROGATION

Is the asking of a question for the purpose of asserting the reverse
of what is asked.

Often, in impassioned discourse, men naturally express what
they would affirm or deny in interrogation.

Assume the proper spirit of the piece, give it an appropriate
tone and action and pause at the end of the question, as if you
waited an answer.

EXAMPLES.

1. Who would be a traitor knave?
   Who would fill a coward's grave?
   Who so base as be a slave?
   Traitor! Coward! turn and flee!

2. To purchase heaven, has gold the power?
   Can gold remove the mortal hour?
   In life can love be bought with gold?
   Are friendship's treasures to be sold?

3. Our brethren are already in the field. Why stand we here idle?
What is it that gentlemen wish? What would they have? Is life so
dear, or peace so sweet, as to be purchased at the price of chains and
slavery?

4. Who is here so base that would be a bondman? If any, speak! for him have I offended. Who is here so rude that would not be a Roman? If any, speak! for him have I offended. Who is here so vile that will not love his country? If any, speak! for him have I offended. None! then none have I offended.

5. And shall we think of ratifying the acts of Charles, yet abolish his laws? Those laws which he in our sight repeated, pronounced, enacted? Laws which he valued himself on passing? Laws in which he thought the system of our government was comprehended? Laws which govern our provinces and our trials? Are we, I say, to repeal such laws, yet ratify his acts?

SOLILOQUY

Consists in the language of a person addressing himself.

The expression should indicate that the attention is directed to thoughts within and not to things without.

EXAMPLES.

1. Beautiful!
   How beautiful is all this visible world!
   How glorious in its action and itself!
   But we, who name ourselves its sovereigns, we,
   Half dust, half deity, alike unfit
   To sink or soar—with our mixed essence, make
   A conflict of its elements.

2. Oh, my offense is rank, it smells to heaven!
   It hath the primal eldest curse upon't—
   A brother's murder.—Pray, alas! I cannot,
   Though inclination be as sharp as 'twill;
   My stronger guilt defeats my strong intent,
   And like a man to double business bound,
   I stand and pause where I shall first begin.

PICTURING

Is the formation of ideas in the mind, concerning what we would read or speak.

No subject should elicit better attention than the one before us. It is necessary that there be a mental picture concerning what we would express. The sentiment of a piece should be studied so well that the reader or speaker may have painted on the canvas of his imagination all the circumstances which gave rise to it. *Thus* and *only thus* may the Elocutionist make his efforts *impressive.*

EXAMPLES.

The wind is high—the window shakes;
With sudden start the miser wakes!
Along the silent room he stalks;
Looks back and trembles as he walks!

After the above lines are read questions may be asked in the following manner.

1. Did you hear the window shake?
2. Could you see the miser as he awoke?
3. Did you see him walk across the room?
4. Was it a small or a large room?
5. Was the room silent?
6. Did the miser look back?
7. Did he have a firm step?

By thus exciting questions in the mind, a correct picture may be drawn.

The following will afford excellent practice in picturing.

AN ORDER FOR A PICTURE.

By Alice Cary.

1. O, good painter, tell me true,
    Has your hand the cunning to draw
    Shapes of things that you never saw?
Ay? Well, here is an order for you.

Woods and cornfield a little brown,—
  The picture must not be over-bright,
  Yet all in the golden and gracious light,
Of a cloud when the summer sun is down.

2. Always and always, night and morn,
  Woods upon woods, with fields of corn
    Lying between them, not quite sere,
  And not in the full, thick, leafy bloom;
  When the wind can hardly find breathing room
    Under their tassels,—cattle near,
  Biting shorter the short green grass,
  And a hedge of sumach and sassafras,
  With bluebirds twittering all around,—
  Ah, good painter, you can't paint sound!

3. These and the little house where I was born,
  Low and little and black and old,
  With children, many as it can hold,
  All at the windows, open wide,—
  Heads and shoulders clear outside,
  And fair young faces all ablush;
    Perhaps you may have seen, some day,
    Roses crowding the selfsame way,
  Out of a wilding, wayside bush.

4. Listen closer. When you have done
    With woods and cornfields and grazing herds,
  A lady, the loveliest ever the sun
  Looked down upon, you must paint for me;
  Oh, if I only could make you see
    The clear blue eyes, the tender smile,
  The sovereign sweetness, the gentle grace,
  The woman's smile, and the angel's face
    That are beaming on me all the while!
    I need not speak these foolish words:
  Yet one word tells you all I would say,—
    She is my mother; you will agree
  That all the rest may be thrown away.

5. Two little urchins at her knee
   You must paint, sir; one like me,—
     The other with a clearer brow,
  And the light of his adventurous eyes
  Flashed with boldest enterprise:
     At ten years old he went to sea,—
  God knoweth if he be living now,—
  He sailed on the good ship "Commodore",—
     Nobody ever crossed her track
     To bring us news, and she never came back.
  Ah, 'tis twenty long years and more
  Since that old ship went out of the bay
     With my greathearted brother on her deck:
     I watched him till he shrank to a speck,
  And his face was toward me all the way.
     Bright his hair was, a golden brown,
       The time we stood at our mother's knee;
     That beautiful head, if it did go down,
       Carried sunshine into the sea!

6. Out in the fields one summer night
   We were together, half afraid
  Of the corn-leaves rustling, and of the shade
     Of the high hills, stretching so still and far,—
  Loitering till after the low little light
  Of the candle shone through the open door,
     And, over the haystack's pointed top,
     All of a tremble and ready to drop
       The first half-hour, the great yellow star
     That we, with staring, ignorant eyes,
  Had often and often watched to see
     Propped and held to its place in the skies
     By the fork of a tall mulberry tree,
  Which close in the edge of our flax-field grew,—
     Dead at the top,—just one branch full
     Of leaves, notched round, and lined with wool,
  From which it tenderly shook the dew
     Over our heads, when we came to play
     In its handbreadth of shadow, day after day,
       Afraid to go home, sir; for one of us bore
  A nest full of speckled and thin-shelled eggs,—

The other, a bird, held fast by the legs,
Not so big as a straw of wheat:
The berries we gave her she would not eat,
But cried and cried, till we held her bill,
So slim and shining to keep her still.

7. At last we stood at our mother's knee.
    Do you think, sir, if you try,
    You can paint the look of a lie?
      If you can, pray have the grace
      To put it solely in the face
    Of the urchin that is likest me;
    I think 'twas solely mine, indeed:
    But that's no matter,—paint it so;
      The eyes of our mother—(take good heed)—
      Looking not on the nest-full of eggs,
    Nor the fluttering bird, held so fast by the legs,
    But straight through our faces, down to our lies,
    And oh, with such injured, reproachful surprise,
  I felt my heart bleed where that glance went as though
    A sharp blade struck through it.

8.   You, sir, know,
    That you on the canvas are to repeat
    Things that are fairest, things most sweet,—
    Woods and cornfields and mulberry tree,—
    The mother,—the lads, with their birds at her knee;
      But, oh, that look of reproachful woe!
    High as the heavens your name I'll shout,
    If you paint me the picture and leave that out.

TRANSITION

Is the change from one intonation to another.

No production is free from change of expression. Therefore, the student should have frequent practice in running from one modulation to another.

The following exercise should be practiced until every needful variety is mastered.

EXAMPLES.

1.

Natural. From the chamber, clothed in white,
The bride came forth on her wedding night;
Low. There in that silent room below,
The dead lay in his shroud of snow.

2.

Effusive. The day is cold, and dark, and dreary;
It rains, and the wind is never weary.
Expulsive. Now by the lips of those ye love, fair gentlemen of France,
Charge for the golden lilies—upon them with the lance!
Explosive. *Quick! quick!* brave spirits, to his rescue fly;
Up! Up! by Heavens! This hero must not die!

3.

Natural. Has your hand the cunning to draw
Shapes of things that you never saw?
Slow. When Ajax strives some rock's vast weight to throw,
The line, too, labors, and the words move slow;
Fast. Not so, when swift Camilla scours the plain,
Flies o'er the unbending corn, and skims along the plain.

4.

Orotund. By Nebo's lonely mountain,
On this side Jordan's wave,
In a vale in the land of Moab,
There lies a lonely grave.
Tremulous. Pity the sorrows of a poor old man,
Whose trembling limbs have borne him to your door;
Whose days are dwindled to the shortest span;
Oh, give relief! and heaven will bless your store.
Subdued. Soft is the strain when zephyrs gently blow,
And the smooth stream in smoother numbers flow;
High. But when loud surges lash the sounding shore,
The hoarse rough verse should like the torrent roar.

5.

Aspirate. Hush! hark! did stealing steps go by?
Came not faint whispers near?
Simple Pure. No!—The wild wind hath many a sigh
Amid the foliage sere.

6.

Natural.	Oh! Mona's waters are blue and bright When the sun shines out like a gay young lover
Low.	But Mona's waters are dark as night When the face of heaven is clouded over.

7.

Slow.	The sun hath set in folded clouds, Its twilight rays are gone;
Low.	And gathered in the shades of night The storm is rolling on.
Effusive.	Alas how ill that bursting storm The fainting spirit braves, When they, the lovely and the lost, Are gone to early graves!

8.

Gradually.	How soft the music of those village bells,
Softer.	Falling at intervals upon the ear In cadence sweet! now dying all away,
Gradually.	Now pealing loud again, and louder still,
Louder.	Clear and sonorous as the gale comes on.

9.

Natural.	I hear them marching o'er the hill,
Monotone.	I hear them fainter, fainter still! I hear them marching o'er the hill, I hear them fainter, fainter still!
High.	They stole, they stole, they stole my child away.
Monotone.	They stole, they stole, they stole my child away!

10.

Heavy.	The combats deepen. On, ye brave, Who rush to glory, or the grave!
Subdued.	Ah! few shall part where many meet! The snow shall be their winding sheet, And every turf beneath their feet Shall be a soldier's sepulchre.

11.

Sim. Pure.	A thousand hearts beat happily; and when Music arose with its voluptuous swell, Soft eyes looked love to eyes which spake again, And all went merry as a marriage-bell;—
Aspirate.	But hush! hark! a deep sound strikes like a rising knell!

12.

Effusive.	Father of earth and heaven! I call thy name!

Orotund.   Round me the smoke of battle rolls;
      My eyes are dazzled with the rustling flame;—
      Father, sustain an untried soldier's soul.

Expulsive. Now for the fight—now for the cannon peal—
      Forward—through blood and cloud and toil and fire!

13.

Gradually. The lingering ray

Lower.   Of dying day
      Sinks deeper down and fades away.

Gradually. A faint light gleams

Louder.   A light that seems
      To grow and grow till nature teems.

14.

Explosive. Rise! rise! ye wild tempests, and cover his flight!

Effusive. 'Tis finished. Their thunders are hushed on the moors,
      Culloden is lost, and my country deplores.

Explosive. The double, double, double beat
      Of the thundering drum,

Loud.   Cries, Hark! the foes come;

Very Loud. Charge, charge! 'tis too late to retreat.

Effusive. The soft complaining flute,
      In dying notes discovers
      The woes of hapless lovers;
      Whose dirge is whispered by the warbling lute.

15.

Sim. Pure. But gentler now the small waves glide
      Like playful lambs o'er the mountain's side,

Orotund. So stately her bearing, so proud her array,
      The main she will traverse forever and aye.
      Many ports will exult at the gleam of her mast!

Aspirate. Hush! hush! thou vain dreamer! this hour is the last.

16.

Gradually. Ever, as on they bore, more loud,

Louder.   And louder rang the pibrock proud,

Gradually. At first the sound, by distance tame,

More   Mellowed, along the waters came:

Gentle.   And lingering long by cape and bay,
      Wailed every harsher note away;

Loud.   When bursting bolder on the ear,
      The clan's shrill gathering they could hear,—
      Those thrilling sounds, that call the night
      Of old Clan-Alpine to the fight.

17.

Pure Asp. Hark! below the gates unbarring!
Tramp of men and quick commands!

Natural. "'Tis my lord come back from hunting."
And the duchess claps her hands.

Slow. Slow and tired came the hunters;
Stopped in darkness in the court.

Fast. "Ho, this way, ye laggard hunters!
To the hall! what sport, what sport!"

Slow. Slow they entered with their master;
In the hall they laid him down.

Vocal Asp. On his coat were leaves and blood stains,
On his brow an angry frown.

18.

Natural. Maud Muller, on a summer's day,
Raked the meadows sweet with hay.

Heavy. Impregnable their front appears,
All horrent with projected spears.

High. "Ye purifying waters, swell!"
Rang out the clear-toned Baptist bell.

Low. 'Tis midnight's holy hour—and silence now
Is brooding, like a gentle spirit, o'er
The still and pulseless world.

Effusive. How often, oh, how often,
In the days that had gone by,
I had stood on the bridge at midnight
And gazed on that wave and sky.

Expulsive. Now, by the lips of those ye love, fair gentlemen of France,
Charge for the golden lilies—upon them with the lance!

Explosive. *Strike*—till the last armed foe expires,
STRIKE—for your altars and your fires,
STRIKE—for the green graves of your sires,
GOD—AND YOUR NATIVE LAND!

19.

High. Once more unto the breach, dear friends, once more
Or close the wall up with English dead!

Natural.	In peace, there's nothing so becomes a man,
	As modest stillness and humility;
High.	But when the blast of war blows in our ears,
	Then imitate the action of the tiger;
Heavy.	Stiffen the sinews, summon up the blood,
	Disguise fair nature with hard favored rage.
Very High.	ON, ON you noble English,
	Whose blood is fetched from fathers of war-proof!
	Fathers, that, like so many Alexanders,
	Have, in these parts, from morn till even fought,
	And sheathed their swords for lack of argument.
Fast.	I see you stand like greyhounds in the slips,
	Straining upon the start. The game 's afoot;
	Follow your spirits, and, upon this charge,
Very High.	CRY—HEAVEN FOR HARRY! ENGLAND! AND ST. GEORGE!

GROUPING

Consists in the arrangement of words.

The words should be grouped and emphasized according to their prominence.

EXAMPLES.

1. Go PREACH *to the coward*, thou death-telling seer!
   OR, if gory Colloden so dreadful appear,
   DRAW, dotard *around thy old wavering sight*,
   This MANTLE, *to cover the phantoms of fright.*

2. HIGH on a THRONE of ROYAL state, which FAR
   Outshone the WEALTH of ORMUS and of IND
   Or WHERE the gorgeous east, with richest hand
   SHOWERS on her kings, Barbaric pearls and gold,
   SATAN exalted sat.

3. Setting aside his high blood's royalty,
   And let him be no kinsman to my liege.

I do DEFY him and I SPIT at him,
Call him—a SLANDEROUS COWARD, and a VILLAIN;
Which to maintain, I would allow him odds,
And meet him were I tied to run a-foot,
Even to the frozen *regions* of the *Alps*,
Or *any other ground* inhabitable,
Wherever *Englishman* durst set his foot.
Meantime let this defend my royalty;
By ALL MY HOPES most falsely doth he LIE.

TRILLED "R"

When immediately followed by a vowel sound, "R" may be trilled in light description, Impersonation and Imitative Modulation.

CLIMAX

Is the extreme point of an increasing emphatic scale.

EXAMPLES.

1. Days, *months*, YEARS, and AGES shall circle away.

2. The battle, sir, is not to the strong alone; it is to the *vigilant*, the ACTIVE, the BRAVE.

3. If I were an American, as I am an Englishman, while a foreign troop remained in my country I never would lay down my arms; no *never*, NEVER, NEVER.

4. What a piece of work is man! How noble in reason! How infinite in faculties! In *form* and *moving, how express and admirable!* In *action*, how like ANGEL! In APPREHENSION, how like a GOD!

REPOSE

Is reserved power which is immeasurable.

Nature has her reserved forces, the knowledge of which impresses us more than her grandest displays of material power. Her mightiest operations are performed in silence, and the effect is deepened and intensified by the sense of a greater power behind that which we see or feel.

Art, too, touches us with its reserved power. There are paintings whose meaning lies on the surface and is exhausted by a single look; and there are others which disappoint at first, yet, reverently studied, gradually glow with beauty, disclosing new marvels of skill, and hidden depths of meaning at each examination, till at last the genius of the artist stands confessed, and you gaze transfixed as by a mighty enchanter.

Indeed, power exerted, however great, never impresses us in the profoundest degree, unless we feel that behind it there is a power greater than itself, by which it can be at any moment augmented. The force that is exhausted in a single effort inspires but a limited degree of admiration.

It has been truly said that the great orator is not he who exhausts his subject and himself at every effort, but he whose expressions suggest a region of thought, a dim vista of imagery, an oceanic depth of feeling, beyond what is compassed by his sentences.

IMITATIVE MODULATION

Is the imitation of things by sound.

Nothing adds more to impressive speech than the play upon words. The sound should correspond to the sense, to have proper effect. In speaking of the *howling* of a dog; the *roaring* of a storm; the *buzz* of a bee; the *crawling* of a snail or the *hiss* of the serpent, the likeness of the sound and the idea is apparent.

EXAMPLES.

1. *March of Soldiers.*

And the measured tread of the grenadiers,
Marching down to their boats on the shore.

2. *Sound of Bell.*

"Ye purifying waters swell!"
In mellow tones rang out a bell.

3. *Sound of Bugle.*

Blow, bugle, blow; set the wild echoes flying;
Blow, bugle; answer, echoes, dying, dying, dying.

4. *Flowing Waters.*

Rivers that run through green meadows
Warble as they flow.

5. *Hum of Insects.*

The slothful beetle with his drowsy hum
Hath rung night's yawning peal.

6. *Step of a Giant.*

With sturdy steps came stalking on his sight
A hideous giant, horrible and high.

7. *Harsh Noise.*

On a sudden open fly
The infernal gates, and on their hinges grate
Harsh thunder!

8. *Wailing of the wind.*

While a low and melancholy moan
Mourns for the glory that hath flown.

9. *Display of Elemental Power.*

Such bursts of horrid thunder,
Such groans of roaring winds and rain, I never
Remember to have heard.

10. *Whisper of Leaves.*

Then crept
A little noiseless noise among the leaves,
Born of the very sight that silence heaves.

11. *Movement of Monsters.*

Part huge of bulk,
Walking unwieldy, enormous in their gait,
Tempest the ocean.

12. *Harsh and Quiet Sounds.*

Two craggy rocks projecting to the main,
The roaring wind's tempestuous rage restrain;
Within, the waves in softer murmurs glide,
And ships secure without their halsers ride.

13. *Language Compared to an Organ.*

O, how our organ speaks with its many and wonderful voices,—
Play on the soft lute of love, blow the loud trumpet of war,
Sing with the high sesquialtro, or, drawing its full diapson,
Shake all the air with a grand storm of its pedals and stops.

IMPERSONATION

Is the imitation of persons by sound.

Children's Voices Are Impersonated By,

1. Voice often ascends and descends.
2. Much interest is expressed.
3. Subdued Force is employed.
4. Voice appears to be in front of mouth.

Voice Of Old Age Is Impersonated By,

1. Voice often ascends and descends.
2. Subdued Force, High Pitch and Slow Rate.
3. Lower Jaw drawn back.
4. Under lip drawn over the teeth.

EXAMPLES.

1. *Spanish.*

Cierto artifice pinto.
Una lucha en que valiente
Un hombre ton solamente
A un horrible leon venicio;

2. *Scotch.*

O, Margaret! My bonnie, bonnie Margaret!
Gie in, gie in, my bairnie, dinna ye drown,
Gie in, and tak' the oath!

3. *Indian.*

Blaze with your seried columns!
I will not bend the knee!
The shackles ne'er again shall bind
The arm which now is free.

4. *Irish.*

And sure, I was tould to come in till yer honor,
To see would ye write a few lines to me Pat;
He's gone for a soger is Misther O'Connor,
Wid a sthripe on his arm, and a band on his hat.

5. *German.*

I'm a broken-hearted Deutcher
Dot's filled mit grief und shame;
I dells you vot der drobles ish—
I does not know my name.

6. *African.*

We has no ark to dance afore, like Isrul's prophet King;
We has no harp to soun' de chords, to help us out to sing;

But 'cordin' to de gif's we has we does de bes' we knows,
An' folks don't 'spise de vi'let-flow'r bekase it aint de rose.

7. *Child.*

Please, Desus, 'et Santa Taus tum down to-night
And b'ing us some p'easents before it is 'ight;
I want he should dive me a nice 'ittle sed,
With b'ight shiny 'unners, and all painted yed;
A box full of tandy, a book and a toy,—
Amen; and then, Desus, I'll be a dood boy.

8. *Old Age.*

These tattered clothes my poverty bespeak,
    These hoary locks proclaim my lengthened years;
And many a furrow in my grief-worn cheek,
    Has been the channel to a flood of tears.

9. *Female.*

Come over, come over the river to me,
If ye are my laddie, bold Charlie Machree.
I see him, I see him. He's plunged in the tide,
His strong arms are dashing the big waves aside.

10. *Yankee.*

Draw up the papers, lawyer, and make 'em good and stout,
For things at home are cross-ways and Betsey and I are out—
We who have lived together so long as man and wife,
Must pull in single harness the rest of our nat'ral life.

EXERCISES FOR PRACTICE IN THE PASSIONS.

PATHOS.

I am all alone in my chamber now
And the midnight hour is near,
And the fagot's crack and the clock's dull tick
Are the only sounds I hear;

And over my soul in its solitude
Sweet feelings of sadness glide,
And my heart and my eyes are full when I think
Of the little boy that died.

TRANQUILITY.

O the snow, the beautiful snow!
Filling the sky and earth below!
Over the housetops, over the street,
Over the heads of the people you meet.

GRAVE.

O, why should the spirit of mortal be proud?
Like a swift-flying meteor, a fast-flying cloud,
A flash of the lightning, a break of the wave,
Man passes from life to his rest in the grave.

GAY.

O, young Lochinvar is come out of the west!
Through all the wide border his steed was the best,
And save his good broadsword he weapons had none,
He rode all unarmed, he rode all alone.
So faithful in love, and so dauntless in war,
There never was knight like the young Lochinvar.

REVERENCE.

Father, thy hand
Hath reared these venerable columns; Thou
Did'st weave this verdant roof. Thou didst look down
Upon the naked earth, and forthwith rose
All these fair ranks of trees.

JOY.

I saw a lady yesterday,
A regular M. D.,

Who 'd taken from the faculty
    Her medical degree;
And I thought if ever I was sick
    My doctor she should be.

SURPRISE.

My Father's trade! Now really, that's too bad!
My Father's trade! Why, blockhead, are you mad?
My father, sir, did never stoop so low—
He was a *gentleman*, I'd have you know.

RESIGNATION.

"Farewell"! said he, "Minnehaha!
Farewell, O my Laughing Water!
All my heart is buried with you,
All my thoughts go onward with you!
Come not back again to labor,
Come not back again to suffer,
Where the famine and the fever
Wear the heart and waste the body."

GRIEF.

My hair is gray but not with years,
        Nor grew it white
        In a single night,
As men's have grown from sudden fears;
My limbs are bowed though not with toil,
        But rusted with a vile repose.

DEFIANCE.

Back, ruffians, back! nor dare to tread
Too near the body of my dead;
Nor touch the living boy; I stand
Between him and your lawless band.

SADNESS.

Alone in the dreary, pitiless street,
With my torn old dress, and bare, cold feet,
All day have I wandered to and fro,
Hungry and shivering and nowhere to go;
The night 's coming on in darkness and dread,
And the chill sleet beating upon my bare head.

SECRECY.

Soldiers, you are now within a few steps of the enemies' outposts. Our scouts report them slumbering around their watchfires, and entirely unprepared for our attack. Let every man keep the strictest silence, under pain of instant death.

ANGER.

And dar'st thou, then, go beard the lion in his den,
The Douglass in his hall?
And hop'st thou hence unscatched to go?
No! by Saint Bride of Bothwell, no!

COMMAND.

"Be that word our sign of parting,
Bird or fiend!" I shrieked upstarting—
"Get thee back into the tempest
And the nights' Plutonian shore!"

SCORN.

The atrocious crime of being a young man. I shall neither attempt to palliate or deny but content myself with hoping that I may be one of that number whose follies cease with their youth and not of that number who are ignorant in spite of age and experience.

TRIUMPH.

Hurrah! the foes are moving! Hark to the mingled din
Of fife, and steed, and trump, and drum, and roaring culverin!
The fiery duke is pricking fast across St. Andre's plain,
With all the hireling chivalry of Guelders and Almayne,
Now by the lips of those ye love, fair gentlemen of France,
Charge for the golden lilies—upon them with the lance!

HUNGER.

Give me three grains of corn, mother,
Only three grains of corn;
'Twill keep the little life I have,
Till the coming of the morn.

JEALOUSY.

I do mistrust thee, woman! and each word
Of thine stamps truth on all suspicions heard.
Borne in his arms through fire from yon Serai—
Say, wert thou lingering there with him to fly?
Thou needs't not answer, thy confession speaks,
Already reddening on thy guilty cheeks!

TERROR.

Alack! I am afraid they have awaked,
And 'tis not done; the attempt and not the deed,
Confound us! Hark! I laid their daggers ready;
He could not miss them.

EXULTATION.

Go ring the bells and fire the guns
And fling the starry banners out;
Shout freedom! till your lisping ones
Give back the cradle-shout.

REVENGE.

And Caesar's spirit, ranging for revenge,
With Ate by his side, come hot from hell,
Shall in these confines with a monarch's voice,
Cry *Havoc*, and let slip the dogs of war!

FEAR.

Hark! I hear the bugles of the enemy! They are on their march along the bank of the river. We must retreat instantly, or be cut off from our boats. I see the head of their column already rising over the height. Our only safety is in the screen of this hedge.

ODE ON THE PASSIONS.

By William Collins.

When MUSIC, heavenly maid, was young,
While yĕt in early Greece she sung,
The Passions ŏft, to hear her shell,
Thrŏnged around her magic cell,—
Exulting, trembling, raging, fainting,—
Possessed beyŏnd the Muse's painting;
By turns they felt the glowing mind
Disturbed, delighted, raised, refined:
Till once, 'tis said, when all were fired,
Filled with fury, rapt, inspired,
From the suppŏrting myrtles round
They snatched her instruments of sound;
And, as they oft had heard apart
Sweet lessons of her fōrceful art,
Each—for MADNESS ruled the hour—
Would prove his own expressive power.

First FEAR, his hand, its skill to try,
 Amid the chords bewildered laid;
And back recoiled, he knew not why,
 E'en at the sound himself had made.—

Next ANGER rushed—his eyes on fire,
 In lightnings owned his secret stings:
In one rude clash he struck the lyre,
 And swept, with hŭrried hands, the strings.—

With woful measures, wan DESPAIR—
 Low sullen sounds!—his grief beguiled;
A solemn, strănge, and mingled air;
 'Twas sad, by fits—by starts, 'twas wild.

But thou, O HOPE! with eyes so fair—
 What was thy delighted mĕasure?
 Still it whispered promised plĕasure,
And băde the lovely scenes at distance hail!
 Still would her touch the strain prolŏng;
And, from the rocks, the woods, the vale,
 She called on ECHO still, through all her sŏng;
And where her swēetèst theme she chose,
 A sŏft responsive voice was heard at every close;
And HOPE, enchanted, smiled, and waved her golden hair.

And lŏnger had she sung—but, with a frown,
 REVENGE impatient rose.
He threw his blood-stained swōrd in thunder down;
  And, with a withering look,
  The war-denouncing trumpet took,
And blew a blast so loud and dread,
 Were ne'er prophetic sounds so full of woes;
  And ever and anon he beat
  The doubling drum with furious heat;
And though, sometimes, each dreary pause between,

Dejected PITY, at his side,
Her soul-subduing voice applied,
Yĕt still he kept his wild unaltered mien;
While each strained ball of sight seemed bursting from his
head.

Thy numbers, JEALOUSY, to naught were fixed—
Sad proof of thy distressful state!
Of differing themes the veering sōng was mixed;
And now it courted LOVE—now, raving called on HATE.—
With eyes upraised, as one inspired,
Pale MELANCHOLY sat retired;
And, from her wild, sequestered seat,
In notes by distance, made more sweet,
Pōured through the mellōw horn her pensive soul;
And, dashing sŏft from rocks around,
Bubbling runnels joined the sound;
Through glades and glooms the mingled mĕasure stole;
Or, ō'er some haunted streams, with fond delay,—
Round a holy calm diffusing,
Love of peace, and lonely musing,—
In hollōw murmurs died away.

But oh! how altered was its sprightlier tone,
When CHEERFULNESS, a nymph of healthiëst hue,
Her bow across her shoulder flung,
Her buskins gemmed with morning dew
Blew an inspiring air, that dale and thicket rung.
The hunter's call, to Faun and Dryad known!
The oak-crowned sisters, and their chaste-eyed queen,
Satyrs, and sylvan boys, were seen,
Peeping from forth their alleys green;
Brown EXERCISE rejoiced to hear;
And Sport leaped up, and seized his beechen spear.

Last came JOY's ecstatic trial:
He, with viny crown, advancing,
First to the lively pipe his hand addressed;
But soon he saw the brisk awakening viol,
Whose sweet entrancing voice he loved the best.
   They would have thought, who heard the strain,
    They saw in Tempe's vale, her native maids,
    Amid the festal-sounding shades,
   To some unwearied minstrel dancing;
   While, as his flying fingers kissed the strings,
LOVE framed with MIRTH a gay, fantastic round—
Loose were her tresses seen, her zone unbound;
    And he, amid his frolic play,
    As if he would the charming air repay,
Shook thousand odors from his dewy wings.

CALISTHENICS

Are gymnastic exercises for the cultivation of physical strength and free and graceful movement.

Calisthenics were held in high esteem by the ancient Greeks and Romans. Muscular elasticity is highly necessary and even indispensible to a proper production of tone. Muscular force can only be acquired by frequent calisthenic drills. Much practice in the following exercises will make grace, strength, and elasticity of body natural.

Avoid a *feeble, unmeaning manner* and enter into the exercise with *life* and *energy*.

RULES FOR POSITION AND MOVEMENT.

1. Heels placed together.
2. Feet forming an angle of 90°.
3. Head should be kept erect.

4. Shoulders and hips thrown back.

5. Chest should be expanded.

6. Hands at side unless otherwise mentioned.

7. Hands clinched unless otherwise specified.

8. All thrusts are from the chest unless otherwise specified.

EXERCISE I.—HAND MOVEMENT.

Throw right hand from chest 4 times; left 4 times; alternate 4 times; simultaneous 4 times. For the outward beats count the numerals from 1 to 16 and on each return pronounce the word "and". Hands supine except when on chest.

1. *Thrust hands downward.*

2. *Thrust hands laterally.*

3. *Thrust hands upward.*

4. *Thrust hands to front.*

5. *Thrust right hand down and up alternately through 8 beats.*

6. *Thrust left hand down and up alternately through 8 beats.*

7. *Alternate, right going down as left goes up, and vice versa 8 counts each.*

8. *Simultaneous, both down, then both up through 8 counts.*

9. *Thrust right hand to right and left alternately through 8 counts.*

10. *Thrust left hand to right and left alternately through 8 counts.*

11. *Thrust both hands alternately to right and left, through 8 counts.*

12. *Thrust both hands to right and left 4 counts each.*

13. *Thrust hands to floor, not bending knees, through 4 beats; then over head, through 4 beats, rising on tiptoe.*

EXERCISE II.—ARM MOVEMENTS.

Hands easily at side.   Count as in Exercise I.

1. *Thrust stiff right arm forward over head through four counts; left through 4 counts.*

2. *Alternate through 8 counts.*

3. *Simultaneous through 8 counts.*

4. *Thrust stiff right arm sideways over head through 4 counts; left through 4 counts.*

5. *Alternate through 8 counts.*

6. *Simultaneous through 8 counts.*

EXERCISE III.—BODY MOVEMENT.

Hands on hips.   Count as in Exercise I.

1. *Bend body to right through 4 counts.*

2. *Bend body to left through 4 counts.*

3. *Alternate through 8 counts.*

4. *Bend body forward 4 times.*

5. *Bend body backward 4 times.*

6. *Alternate through 8 counts.*

7. *Twist body half 'round to right four times.*

8. *Twist body half 'round to left 4 times.*

9. *Alternate through 8 counts.*

10. *Bend body to right, back, left, front; then reverse,—bending to left, back, right, front.*

EXERCISE IV.—HEAD MOVEMENTS.

Count as in Exercise I.

1. *Throw the head forward through 4 counts.*
2. *Throw the head backward through 4 counts.*
3. *Alternately through 8 counts.*
4. *Throw the head to the right through 4 counts.*
5. *Throw the head to the left through 4 counts.*
6. *Alternately through 8 counts.*

EXERCISE V.—DUMB-BELL MOVEMENT.

Close hands on chest. Count as in Exercise I.

1. *Throw both hands downward through 4 counts.*
2. *Throw both hands laterally through 4 counts.*
3. *Throw both hands upward through 4 counts.*
4. *Throw both hands to front through 4 counts.*
5. *Throw both hands to the right through 4 counts.*
6. *Throw both hands to the left through 4 counts.*
7. *Throw right hand upward, left hand downward through 8 counts.*
8. *Throw left hand upward, right hand downward through 8 counts.*

EXERCISE VI.—CLAPPING EXERCISE.

Close hands on chest.

Throw out right hand twice, left twice, both together 4 times, and clap hands four times.

1. *Front.*
2. *Laterally.*

3. *Upward.*

4. *Downward.*

EXERCISE VII.—SWAYING SWINGING ARMS.

1. *Stamp left foot, then right; Charge diagonally forward with right; Bend and straighten right knee; at same time throwing arms back from horizontal in front.*

2. *Same as No. 1, on left side.*

3. *Same as No. 1, diagonally backward on right side.*

4. *Same as No. 1, diagonally backward on left side.*

EXERCISE VIII.—RAISING SHOULDERS.

Hands at side.   Count as in Exercise I.

1. *Raise right shoulder through 4 counts.*

2. *Raise left shoulder through 4 counts.*

3. *Alternate through 8 counts.*

4. *Simultaneous through 8 counts.*

EXERCISE IX.—ATTITUDES.

1. *Hands on hips, stamp left foot, then right; Charge diagonally forward with right, looking over left shoulder.*

2. *Same as No. 1, diagonally forward, left foot.*

3. *Same as No. 1, diagonally back, right.*

4. *Same as No. 1, diagonally back, left.*

24827014R00061

Printed in Great Britain
by Amazon